What People Are Saying About

Why Don't They Just Q

"I read all of my Al-Anon books, attend meetings, and I have a wonderful church family, but this book presents some new thoughts to me. It's wonderful and has proven to be of great solace. . . . as if you've been here in my home, observing."

—Rosemary L., Anderson, Indiana

"[This book] will be valued by many, many people. A very meaningful gift of God's grace to families who need sanity in the middle of their runaway insanity."

—Mike Richards Jr., Director of Recovery Ministries, International Bible Society

"My association with The Salvation Army for over forty-nine years, allows me to confirm the importance of Joe's practical approach to addiction and recovery."

—Lt. Colonel Clarence Harvey, The Salvation Army, Kansas City, Missouri

"…stayed up late last night reading it; inspiring! This book is for people like me; with chemically addicted people in their life . . . one of the most clear/helpful guides to learn how to navigate the confusion, drama and pain associated with addiction in a family. Passionate, humble, full of wisdom . . . a must read for the addicted and those who care about them."

—Donna Schwartz, MFT, CAC III, Valley Hope Treatment Services in Colorado

"Solid, helpful and hopeful . . . as a Pastor who deals constantly with those heartbroken by addictions and as the son of an alcoholic parent, I highly recommend *Why Don't They Just Quit?* to others inside or outside a community of faith. Joe knows that his sobriety didn't come just on his own strength, but through the power of a dynamic relationship with Christ, his "higher power" often mentioned in AA."

— Rick Bundschuh, author, cartoonist and pastor of Kauai Christian Fellowship, Kauai, Hawaii

"Articulate, 'real-world' practical, thoroughly 'user friendly' and strongly recommended."

—James A. Cox, Editor-in-Chief/Midwest Book Review

"I absolutely could not put the book down! It was amazing to me that someone could write something that I had lived with almost to the T. It gave me understanding from a different perspective, enlightening me to different ways of seeing the disease. It saved my sanity."

—S. Chism, Maui, Hawaii

"I know Joe and he has immense personal credibility to address the confusing, complex issue of addiction. This book is surprisingly clear, crisp and candid. Many in our congregation, community and nation need to read what Joe has to say."

—Alan Ahlgrim, Lead Pastor Rocky Mountain Christian Church, Niwot, Colorado

"Just got my book. I'm previewing it and hit a, "Thank you, Lord!" moment when reading about raising the bottom. I've wondered about that idea for some time now, but couldn't seem to find professionals nor support groups who I felt were smart enough to answer my questions. Bless you all for putting out these resources!"

—Robb B., Pineville, North Carolina

"Many reading this book are facing the battle of your life. Alcohol and drugs consumed my daughter's life. I can't put into words—the anguish of attending my daughter's funeral. I wish I had this book long ago. Maybe Mia would still be here. I didn't know how to help her. *Why Don't They Just Quit?* is full of answers I could have used."

—Pam M., Niwot, Colorado

"…a must read not only for families of addicts and alcoholics looking for answers, but for anyone who has been intrigued by irrational compulsions and wondered how recovery takes place. I consider *Why Don't They Just Quit?* to be one of the top five recovery books for families and I anticipate it being widely used by treatment programs throughout the country."

—Nicolas Taylor, Ph.D., National Expert on the Treatment of Methamphetamine Addiction

"…I read your book twice. I thought I knew quite a bit about alcohol addiction but in reality, I probably only knew 20% before reading your book."

—C.H., Denver, Colorado

"Joe writes with authority and clarity . . . . Its straightforwardness and intimacy as well as its lack of pretense give it a veracity, that is genuine . . . an excellent read for family and friends as well as the recovering person."

—James W. Russell, M.D., FACP American Society of Addiction Medicine
former director of Founder's Hall Treatment Center, St. Johnsbury, VT

"Joe explains addiction and recovery in terms we all can understand. We recommend it to all the families at our center."

—Lee Barchan, Executive Director, Transitions Recovery, North Miami Beach, Florida

"As a recovering person myself, I found this book to be full of facts useful in sharing with visitors at our weekly meetings. I especially appreciate that Joe included the spiritual part of recovery and most importantly, the underlying message that anyone can recover—bringing hope to those seeking direction."

—Vicki Beatty, Celebrate Recovery Leader, Covenant Chapel, Leawood, Kansas

"Everything you've always wanted and needed to know about addiction and recovery is explained clearly and honestly in this amazingly compassionate, yet straightforward book. If you know someone who is struggling with addiction and don't know how to help them, read this book. All the answers you seek are here."

—Michael Z, M.A., author, The Wisdom of the Rooms, A Year of Weekly Reflections

"...a very good read. Joe effectively draws together much of the wisdom from AA and Al-Anon's 70-plus years of experience, the hands-on lessons from professional counseling and the more recent medical advances in the treatment of addictions. His counsel and advice, while based on complicated problems with no easy answers is very practical and down to earth."

—Dave Ketter, LCP, Clinical Supervisor/Valley Hope Association

"...vital advice, procedures and hope...This book offers workable, detailed solutions, with answers to common questions about this problem and offers hope to family and friends. A unique work providing new insights."

—Lightword Publishing Book Review

"There is a tug-of-war going on in the recovery community between those with academic letters behind their names and those who have walked through the tunnel of addiction. For example there are those who believe AA is a positive road to walk, while others scorn AA for any number of reasons. Joe writes and talks about addiction with a warmth and depth of understanding that so many others lack. . . . superbly written, a straight-talking, no frills guide."

—Ned Wicker, Addiction Chaplain and Host/Recovery Now! Radio

"Reading this book during the time I was married to an addict would have saved me many days of suffering and stress. Anyone close to an addict should read *Why Don't They Just Quit?*"

—Marilyn Russell, RN, Boulder, Colorado

"Joe combines a lifetime of personal and professional experience dealing with this issue in a practical and highly personal overview. The book is excellent. I wish I had read it a year ago."

—Sheriff Joe Pelle, Boulder County, Colorado

"This factual, fascinating book offers compassion for family members, solid evidence-based information about the disease, answers to commonly asked questions, and most important of all, a sense that you are not alone. Joe's faith and his descriptions of the role faith plays in recovery light up the pages to reveal the essential role of spirituality in recovery. This book is an important and essential resource for family members, teachers, court services personnel, counselors, treatment personnel, ministers, doctors, and anyone whose life is affected by alcohol and other drug use/addiction."

—Kathy Ketcham, coauthor, Teens Under the Influence

"Your story has encouraged and helped me deal with my son's addictions and has given me great peace as a parent. I no longer feel alone under a terrible cloud of guilt; my son's choices have been his own and I as a parent have done all I can. I continue to love him, encourage him and, as far as possible allow him to make his mistakes. I can put away the guilt and the shame, pick up my own pieces and move forward."

— Kathy C., Longmont, Colorado

"I've read several books and literature on alcoholism and this is my favorite. This book tells how to show the addict "tough love" and ways of "raising the bottom" while still loving them and never giving up hope that one day they will "get it.""

—Jessica P., Vacherie, Louisiana

"This is a book that when you start reading it, you can't put it down. Joe is not telling you how to cure addiction, he is telling you pretty much what to expect and what not to expect. I read the book because of my son's addiction. We didn't think it was happening. It helped me to understand what my son must be going through and what to expect. It's a book about real people. A "must read" for all."

—Carla E., Marseilles, Illinois

"…more than the typical self-help book, this book is gritty, honest, and full of practical tips. I loved the myriad quotes sprinkled throughout from such diverse individuals as Mother Theresa, Winston Churchill, Mark Twain, Ozzie Osbourne, and Herzanek's own family members. It is the intimate way in which the author shares himself that lends what could be "just another addiction recovery book" a fresh and hopeful voice. I recommend this for anyone impacted by the effects of addiction."

—Julie McGuire, Associate Editor, The Internet Review of Books

"…one of the most valuable books I've ever read. Having a son with a severe alcohol/drug addiction, who's been through more than one treatment program, I was desperately looking for answers—not hype or glitter. I consider *Why Don't They Just Quit* to be my "Bible" on drug abuse issues. Mr. Herzanek lays it out in a straightforward way, using his and other's personal experiences to clarify the how and why of addiction and recovery. . . a must have tool for anyone impacted by a loved one's addiction."

—Mari N., Burlington, Washington

"After painfully watching my sons struggle with addictions for 10 years and trying desperately to help them, to no avail, this book spoke to me in a manner that no other book on this subject ever did. I contribute Joe's words, to my healing as well. My sons could relate to his book, and it gave them hope too. I recommend this book to anyone caught in the web of addiction—whether it be the addicted or the loved one of an addict.

—Janis P., Brookings, Oregon

"My daughter recently told us she had an alcohol and Vicodin addiction. I didn't know where to turn. A friend loaned me this book and I could not put it down. I read it from front to back in one sitting. It was like all the answers I was asking in my head, were all answered. It was literally a lifesaver for me. I was pretty sure before I read the book that I couldn't handle what was coming next for my daughter. After I read it, I didn't feel so lost and hopeless."

—Sandy T., Marseilles, Illinois

"Thank you, thank you . . . I've been struggling for years to encourage my husband to stop enabling our youngest son. Last weekend he ended up in jail again (thank God) and I took the firmest stand ever and finally convinced my husband to leave him there! Man, it was hard, but the neat thing is that while searching for info about "enabling" he found this book and finally got "it" that we should not bail our son out after reading your sections on enabling! I feel so empowered, not hopeless as before. God bless from Loveland."

—Pat M., Loveland, Colorado

"A thoughtful, caring book written for the everyday person with an addicted loved one; very helpful when you're alone and desperately hoping your loved one is safe because he isn't home and you know he is out using again."

—Karon W., Concord, North Carolina

"God bless you. Al-Anon and AA are a Godsend, but I have found other books to be very general and a little outdated with today's times. Joe's book has answered so many questions for me that I can relate to and put into practice."

—D.B., Lakewood, Colorado

"I was truly touched by Joes's struggles and the way he was able to help his son avoid the very same problems he experienced in early adulthood. Joe opens his life for everyone, helping parents and loved ones recognize warning signs and identify steps to begin the recovery process."

—Michael W., Kansas City, Missouri

"This is a must read...a book about truth, commitment, consequences, and a belief that things can change. It describes the complexity of drug addiction and the scars it leaves, along with practical solutions that can be implemented today."

—Magistrate Judge Tijani R. Cole, Ph.D., J.D., Boulder, Colorado

"…an informative book for anyone interested in how the disease of addiction manipulates and destroys individuals and all the people around them. It delivers a clear and real picture of recovery…a great gift for family, friends and employers as they struggle with their role in the addict's life."

—Frank Lisnow, Executive Director of CeDAR, Denver, Colorado
Colorado Past President of National Association of Addiction Counselors

"Joe's book provides insights and solutions that are proven to work for recovery—not only for the addict but for the entire family system."

—Tony Marquez, VP of Business Development,
Pacific Coast Recovery Center, Laguna Beach, California

Who has woe? Who has sorrow?
Who has strife? Who has complaints?
Who has needless bruises? Who has bloodshot eyes?

Those who linger over wine,
who go to sample bowls of mixed wine.
Do not gaze at wine when it is red,
when it sparkles in the cup,
when it goes down smoothly!

In the end it bites like a snake
and poisons like a viper.
Your eyes will see strange sights
and your mind imagine confusing things.

You will be like one sleeping on the high seas,
lying on top of the rigging.
"They hit me," you will say, "but I'm not hurt!
They beat me, but I don't feel it!
When will I wake up so I can find another drink?"

—*Proverbs 23:29-35*

*Sooner or later everyone sits down
to a banquet of consequences.*
—*Robert Louis Stevenson*

Why Don't They Just Quit?

What families and friends need to know about addiction and recovery

Joe Herzanek

Published by:

WHY DON'T THEY JUST QUIT?
What families and friends need to know about addiction and recovery

Joe Herzanek

Copyright ©2007, 2010, 2012 by Changing Lives Foundation,
Loveland, CO 80537

Third printing: December 2012
Second printing (revised/updated): January 2010
First printing September 2007

Published by Changing Lives Foundation,
1855 Gemini Ct. • Loveland CO 80537
www.ChangingLivesFoundation.org

All scripture quotations, unless otherwise indicated, are taken from the Holy Bible, New International Version®, NIV®.

www.WhyDontTheyJustQuit.com

Cover Design: Karen Steenekamp • www.opn-dsn.com
Interior Design and Art Direction: Judy Herzanek

ISBN-13: 978-1-481-10669-6
ISBN-10: 1-481-10669-4

Disclaimer: This book is not intended to provide therapy, counseling, clinical advice or treatment or to take the place of clinical advice and treatment from your professional mental health provider or personal physician. It is up to the reader to investigate any healthcare physician regarding mental or medical health issues. Neither the publisher nor the author takes any responsibility for any possible consequences from any treatment, action, or application of information in this book to the reader.

Printed in the USA

Dedication

The right people were there for me when I needed help to push me toward recovery. During my most difficult times, my parents Joe and Gladys didn't give up on me. I wouldn't have blamed them if they did. I pushed them to the limit on many occasions. The same is true for my former wife, Vicki, and my daughter Jami. With time, patience and strength, we have restored our shattered relationships. I'm grateful for their forgiveness.

My wife, Judy, has kept me stable for over twenty-five years. It takes a unique person to live with me day in and day out. She is my best friend and love.

My three wonderful children Jami, Jake and Jessica have played important roles in my life. We have all grown up together.

Many years ago, when I first began this odyssey called *life in recovery,* the counselors at Valley Hope, my treatment center, were there for me at the right place and time. Experiencing their compassion firsthand was a defining moment in my life.

Ernie Simmons, Dick Lane, Steve Aikman, Bob Bennett, Ted Nissen, Russ Minary and Floyd Golf are just some of the men who gave me clarity when I needed it.

I am grateful to the many hundreds of men and women also in recovery, who had just the perfect thing to say when I needed it the most. I will always remember those of you who were willing to share your time, and a portion of your lives, with me. I'm blessed to have had all of you in my life. Your love and friendship, along with the strength I've found in my relationship with the Lord have brought me this far. I'm not at the end of my journey.

Acknowledgments

I want to thank my editors, David Hicks and Tracey Lawrence, for guiding me through this experience and making me sound good on paper. I'm also indebted to my wife Judy, who was locked in a house with me for many months, decoding my scribbles until the wee hours, and who had the patience of Job.

I am grateful for their organization, encouragement, and insights through each step of the process. In all honesty, without their help, writing this book would have been impossible.

Table of Contents

Part 2: It's a Family Affair

Part 3: All About Treatment

Part 4: Life in Recovery

Part 5: Q & A with Joe

Foreword

Our phone rings, and a woman I don't know asks to speak with Joe. Her son is in jail with a DUI again, and she wonders what she can do to "help" him. Joe spends the next forty-five minutes talking to her.

As we are out running errands the next day, an old friend strikes up a conversation. She is concerned about her sister, who is coming to visit and who has a severe drug dependency problem. Joe listens intently and shares his thoughts. Later that same day, as we are getting ready to leave our bible study, someone from our church takes him aside to ask for advice about one of his employees. These encounters, which some might consider interruptions, give Joe great satisfaction and add meaning to his day. Wherever we find ourselves, he is always willing to offer support and empathy. After being married to Joe for more than twenty-five years, I am well aware of his amazing gift. In fact, it was one of the things that first drew me to him.

Joe has a unique way of explaining and simplifying the most complicated problems. People listen to him. Because he personally lived the addict/alcoholic life, he can identify with the condition and lifestyle of the addict. Because he went through a residential treatment program and now has over thirty years of long-term recovery, Joe can speak to people about hope, and testify that recovery is possible. Because my husband spent almost two decades counseling inmates in jails and prisons, he understands the criminal mindset. He knows what works and what doesn't when it comes to addiction and recovery.

Not being afraid to tell people exactly what they need to hear, Joe will clearly tell a mother when her "helping" is actually making the situation worse. He has a keen ear. What seems to be the most hopeless, complicated situation for others has a clear solution for Joe. With wit and ease, he sorts through problems, paring them down to one or two basic issues—which almost always center on someone's substance abuse.

I'm excited that Joe's insights and advice are now available to those in need. I am a recovering person myself. Together we have gathered and answered some of the most common questions, concerns, and myths about substance abuse, recovery, and the role of faith in recovery. We've even added some new Q&A based on the many email questions we receive daily. This is a chance for people to receive clear, practical, no-nonsense information on this topic that can actually help them immediately.

Addiction is a serious disease, which naturally places a heavy burden on families. But Joe brings to this topic a positive outlook and a welcome humor — something you don't normally expect to experience when reading about substance abuse! Although he lived through some very tough times, he managed to survive, and survive with his sense of humor intact. You may come across a funny story or quote and be surprised, since this book is about such a serious topic. What a great testimony to recovery, to be able to laugh again.

Joe speaks from firsthand experience, having survived shattered relationships, a life-threatening disease, physical and mental withdrawal, police problems, and raising two teenagers. He also shares his story of true recovery, restored relationships, renewed health, and spiritual growth.

Although Joe will never forget the serious lessons learned during his lifetime, he has worked through his past and moved on to a new life in recovery. As you read the following pages, Joe's account of his personal struggle with addiction will show you the way to begin this journey as well. If you are a part of a family struggling with substance abuse, life doesn't have to remain complicated and despairing. You and your family can begin a new life today. I'm confident that you too, will be able to laugh again.

— *Judy Herzanek*

Introduction

Congratulations! You have just taken a step toward helping your family member, friend, employee or loved one. The book you are holding in your hands is all about solutions, practical solutions you can use right now to start making positive changes in your own life and in the life of someone you care about.

Addiction—called *America's silent new epidemic* by Larry King of CNN—may be one of the most mysterious problems in our nation today—with approximately one out of ten adults in trouble with alcohol and/or drug use. Although this problem has plagued us for generations, the past few decades have brought about a huge increase in its severity. New drugs and new technologies, enabling stronger addictions, are being developed as I write. An end to this problem is nowhere in sight. In fact, it appears to be getting worse with time. Controversy, myths, shame, stigma, ignorance, and confusion surround this serious topic, and the questions are endless: *Is it a disease or a moral failing? What's the cause? Who's to blame? Is there a cure? Is it a self-inflicted wound or is it in my DNA?*

You may have your own list of questions about recovery:

- *What can I do to help?*
- *Is treatment necessary? And if so, what kind?*
- *How can I afford it?*
- *What happens in twelve-step meetings?*
- *Do twelve-step meetings conflict with my faith?*
- *How can I do an intervention with a rebellious teenager?*
- *How do I survive going through relapse with someone?*
- *Should I talk about this with my friends? What if they stigmatize and pass judgment on my loved one?*
- *With so many theories and methods being offered today, how can I know which theories are true, and which methods work?*
- *Why don't they just quit?*

After more than thirty years of long-term recovery from drugs and alcohol, and seventeen years of work as a certified addiction counselor in jails and prisons, I can answer all these questions, and help you unpack many other issues surrounding the problem of addiction. Through my work with thousands of men, women, and family members struggling to be free of the ravages of this disease, I've gained valuable insights. The interviews I conducted on my *Recovery Television* series, featuring experts in the addiction field combined with substance abuse issues with my own son, continue to shape my life message. This unique combination of personal long-term recovery, parenting teens and counseling experience has given me a platform from which I am able to relate to families and substance abusers from all walks of life.

You probably have fears regarding what hardships will have to happen to someone you care about before he/she will wake up and change. Sometimes a little more knowledge on a topic can give you the motivation and confidence you need to move toward positive change. You are not alone in trying to face this problem—most families are affected at some level by this disease. Substance abusers may have jobs, families, or own their own businesses. They are students, professors, attorneys, employees, truck drivers, police officers, pastors, nurses, sons, daughters, spouses, mothers, and fathers. You may have a spouse, neighbor, co-worker or a teenager battling drug and alcohol abuse. These are real people, living with real families. Addiction is an equal-opportunity destroyer. It respects on one. It doesn't care what level of education a person has. It is insidious. It may strike all at once, or it may slowly slither its way in.

Once addiction has gained access to a life, it will refuse to leave without a fight, and it won't fight fairly. When pushed away, it will patiently wait for the opportunity to strike its victim again when his or her guard is down. Addiction is never satisfied. After it has destroyed health, devastated families, ended careers, and put children in foster homes, it still wants more.

I will be sharing many of my challenges in recovery as well as some true-life accounts from my own family and from those of the people I've counseled. (Out of respect for their privacy, I will change their names and any revealing details.) My hope is to reach families that are discouraged, frustrated, and baffled by the cycle of addiction. *Is it a spiritual problem as well?* Yes. *Can we blame it all on the devil?* No. I'll speak more on that later.

If you are dealing with an addict in your family, you may feel helpless and have tough questions. First, I want to commend you for making efforts to help someone who has lost control of life. You very well may be the catalyst that brings them into successful recovery. I believe you will come away with answers that will help equip you to deal with this problem. When someone is in the midst of turmoil, the road to recovery seems impossible to find. I will guide you to that road, so that you can help your loved one find it—and stay on it.

Throughout this book, I've raised common questions and myths about this deadly disease. My particular story allows me to share candidly from the perspective of one who has battled addiction and achieved long-term success. By debunking these myths, answering these questions and sharing these stories, I hope to show you that freedom from addiction and an enjoyable life in recovery is attainable for anyone. I am just one of millions who have found the way out. Addiction is not a hopeless situation. Every day men, women, and adolescents take their first steps on this journey. Dramatic changes do happen.

I'm honored that you have chosen to read *Why Don't They Just Quit?* I want to say to you with conviction that addicts and alcoholics aren't crazy, and they can quit.

I invite you to explore this topic with me, chapter by chapter, and trust that you will discover practical insights that can make all the difference in the life of someone you care about. I would even encourage you to read this along with a friend or someone else affected by addiction, so that you can discuss it in the community of others.

> *Addicts and alcoholics aren't crazy, and they can quit!*

My best to you and your family as you move a step closer toward long-term recovery.

—*Joe Herzanek*

Part 1

Why Don't They Just Quit?

Chapter 1
A Look at My Life

Why write this book?

Kansas City, 1967:
On a dark summer night, my buddy Doug and I hop the chain-link fence at the end of the airport runway. After smoking some good weed, we sneak through the tall grass, lie on our backs and wait. Soon the ground trembles, the blinding lights of a huge jet flood the area and the deafening sound momentarily shakes our world. The jet is approximately fifty feet above us as it comes in to land—an incredible experience. Life at nineteen is fun.

Kansas City, 1972:
It's about noon. I'm alone in my apartment. Some people were here last night but they left hours ago. I've been snorting coke since yesterday. My sinuses are a mess. I can't inhale or breathe through my nose. I begin to think of ways to solve this problem. A soaking wet washcloth should do the trick. Lying on my back, on the couch, I put some rocks of cocaine in my nose, place the warm, wet washcloth over my face and let the moisture fill my nose and dissolve the drug. Bingo, it works! I'm a genius. Needles are only for drug addicts, so I won't go there—I'm no junkie.

Some family members and a few friends have been bugging me about my "drug problem." I wish they would just mind their own business. I know what I'm doing. Besides, it's not really a problem. I mean, heck, if it was, I'd just quit.

Longmont, Colorado, 2010:

I hate addiction. I hate the way it devestates families. Addiction to alcohol and drugs almost killed me. My life-threatening problem was killing my family as well.

Addiction took sixteen years of my life, and *almost* took it all. I was in bondage to my addiction, and caring people actually helped me to break it. I'm humbled to say I've been free from alcohol and drug abuse for over thirty years. Life is good. The sickness that robbed me of joy, peace, and happiness is now in remission. God has been good to me.

The road to recovery has not always been an easy one. I've had many days of struggle. But although this journey of recovery is tough at times, it is possible not only to survive, but also to enjoy life again. A faithful friend of mine, Dick Lane, used to tell me in my times of adversity, "Every day is not a hot fudge sundae." He's right, of course, and I no longer try to medicate life's challenges. After getting into recovery, I found that helping others was a great way to get my mind off myself. It also made me feel good. And, it's a *genuine feel-good*—not an artificial, drug-induced one.

Through my own quest for knowledge and recovery, I was led to pursue training in the addiction and recovery field. I spent years working in jails and prisons in Colorado, as both a substance abuse counselor and chaplain. As a certified addiction counselor, I've worked with *thousands* of men, women, teens and their families to help them battle addiction. I've learned a lot over the years, as I've listened intently to many recovery stories. Writing this book is the latest step in a logical progression for me, a culmination of my personal experience and life's work.

This chapter of my life—successful recovery—may spark a new hope in you. I believe in the old adage, "You can't keep it unless you give it away." I can't imagine going through such a life struggle without trying to redeem it for some good. Perhaps I can even help you to avoid a mistake that could save your family a lot of needless pain.

This book is about recovery from addiction—recovery for the addict, the family, and close friends. It is also about how to cope with life when you are dealing with addiction in your family, relationships, or the workplace. My own personal battle, my training, and countless hours working with others who are struggling has given me some unique insights. I'm a survivor, a combat veteran of sorts. I want you to know the truth about addiction, answer some of your most perplexing questions, and provide you with practical tools to help those you care about.

> ### Success is to be measured
> ### not so much by the position
> ### that one has reached in life
> ### as by the obstacles which he has overcome.
> —*Booker T. Washington*

My story is not unique, although for years I thought it was. I felt alone, unable to find a way out of a very dark pit. If *I* found my way out of the trenches to recovery, I know that anyone can. It's never too late to start the journey. I don't care who you are or how bad your situation may be.

Dramatic changes are possible. I've seen recovery happen at all ages and stages of life. Teens and adults alike can win this battle. I have seen a seminary professor who waited until he was in his sixties to get help to overcome addiction. He's now well into his seventies and having the time of his life. I've been blessed to hear about, and play a part in, so many lives that have been restored.

Quitting is a moment in time; it is not recovery. The word *recover* means to "restore or bring back from loss, that which has been stolen." My hope for those who read this book is for families to be restored. This all begins with knowledge and awareness. Families have been shattered because of the stronghold of addiction, and many loved ones have walked away not realizing there are options and ways to help the addict. This book is about solutions—what works,

> *Quitting is a moment in time; it is not recovery.*

what doesn't, and why. Life in recovery can be very, very good. It can even be *fun* again—for the whole family.

Chapter 2
Dying for a Cold One

Why do we all take drugs?

From the delivery room to the nursing home, everyone has one thing in common: a desire to increase pleasure and decrease pain. Babies often come into the world crying. They come from the mother's womb (98 degrees) to room temperature (72 degrees), and they are cold. A nurse wraps them in a nice tight blanket and places this fragile life into its mother's arms, now content—until he gets hungry.

We all want comfort at every phase of life. And we don't have to live long to realize that there is always something within us begging to be satisfied. Everyone can relate to this fact of life on some level. Realizing this is a crucial step toward helping your family and friends who are battling addictions.

Here's *the truth* about drugs and alcohol: They are very effective for increasing pleasure or decreasing pain. They really do work, and many of them work fast. You don't have to wait around and look at your watch: you can get instant pleasure or instant pain relief. Their effectiveness feeds into our culture of instant gratification.

So when you talk to your friend or loved one and tell them they need to stop using alcohol and/or drugs (something that has been "working for" them for a long time), don't be shocked when they look at you like *you* are the crazy one! They have a good idea what liv-

> *Drugs are very effective for increasing pleasure or decreasing pain.*

ing life substance-free really means: going through withdrawal, seeking counseling, committing to a treatment program, making new friends, experiencing stress, getting a job, growing up, being responsible, and being a better spouse and parent. To the addict/alcoholic, none of this is going to sound better than using. I know it didn't to me.

One of the big problems for many dependent people (myself included) is that they don't see the problem developing in the beginning. For most men and women, dependence is a slow and gradual process. Some will see their drinking as a reward: *I worked hard today so I'll reward myself with several drinks in the evening*. No one I've known has purposefully set out to become an alcoholic or drug addict. In the beginning, using an addictive substance usually starts out as fun; but in the end, it becomes the very thing that robs their ability to enjoy life.

The dependent person knows how to feel better fast. Alcohol and drug use have become a way of life, a way of dealing with pain and experiencing pleasure. So expect recovery to be a battle—but a battle worth fighting. And I'm here to encourage you to believe that the battle can be won! Those in recovery can and do make dramatic changes in their lives.

> ## *Has he lost his mind?*
> ## *Can he see or is he blind?*
>
> —Ozzy Osborne, *Iron Man*

I spent many years lost in the fog of addiction. Friends and family members all tried to get through to me. I was defiant and wanted to keep using in spite of the fact that it was no longer fun. In fact, fun was a distant memory. It had become all about killing the pain. I see this now only in hindsight. At the time, I just had a chip on my shoulder (a brick, actually), and I didn't even know why.

> *Insanity: doing the same thing*
> *over and over again*
> *and expecting different results.*
> —*Albert Einstein*

The real insanity concerning addiction is the fact that people continue their usage in spite of all the bad consequences. In fact, for me, the consequences were becoming *reasons* to get high. Addiction is a means to escape, and the more you try to escape from reality, the worse reality becomes.

Imagine having a friend who rents a DVD. He brings it home, puts it in his player, and sits back to watch the movie. After about thirty minutes, he decides that the movie is terrible and boring. He pops it out of the machine and puts it back in the case with plans to return it tomorrow—but the plan is always for tomorrow. In about an hour or so, he decides to put it back in the DVD player to try it again. Nothing has changed; it's the same crummy movie. But he keeps thinking that one of these times it will be better. Now, imagine that this scenario goes on for *years*.

This is the insanity of addiction. Each time the addict uses, there is this false hope that life will be better, that using will fix everything, and life won't be so bad. And, for those who witness this crazy behavior, such a pattern makes no sense at all. You feel as if your friend or family member has lost his mind.

Chapter 3
Good Question!

Why don't they just quit?

Several of my TV talk shows on the subject of recovery featured *man on the street* interviews: I would pick some large public place, like a walking mall, and ask people all sorts of questions on the topic. One particularly loaded question was, "How do you become chemically dependent?" A few people had answers right away, but most had to stop and think about it first. Many had no answer at all.

My questions on the street provoked many people, resulting in some interesting responses; some were quite emotional. On one warm summer day we were out asking questions to shoppers on the Pearl Street Mall in Boulder, close to where I live. I approached a woman and asked her the question of the day: *When a person's world starts falling apart because of their substance abuse, why don't they just quit?* She signaled to us that she did not want to answer. So my camera operator and I continued moving along the mall area. Suddenly, she came back to us from behind, yelling, "How dare you ask me something like that!" Maybe my average-woman-on-the-street was taking it a little too personally? Perhaps someone in her family was fighting substance abuse and she felt threatened by this stranger's question. You never know how many in a crowd have experienced the profound pain of addiction. Whatever the issues people are dealing with, I have learned much just by asking this key question.

> *Be kinder than necessary,*
> *for everyone you meet*
> *is fighting some kind of battle.*
>
> —*Unknown*

Some of those I interviewed repeated the question back to me with, "That's a good question, why don't they just quit?" Parents, pastors, spouses, mothers, brothers, friends, police officers, teachers, judges, counselors, and employers all struggle with this same question today. In fact, many addicts and alcoholics themselves can't understand why they continue down this road.

The Recovery Process

So in real life, how hard is it to quit using? And why don't they just quit? Let me start by mentioning a few variables. The length of time someone has been using and how much of the drug they have been using (which affects their tolerance level) are factors in determining the difficulty. The recovery process for a twenty-two-year-old with an alcohol and marijuana problem will be different from that of a forty-two-year-old with a methamphetamine or heroin addiction. To completely stop all use of substances, for either person, will be the most difficult challenge they may ever face. *It is hard to quit—really hard.*

A person's body and central nervous system will experience a jolt, or shock, when they stop using most drugs. This physical consequence of recovery is tough, but usually short-lived—lasting anywhere from a few days to a few weeks. The mental part is a larger battle and will last longer.

It is hard to quit —really hard.

Motivation and desire to change play a big role in the success of a person's recovery. Unfortunately, most people don't want to stop *all* use. Users would much prefer to be able to experience occasional or controlled use. Until they have resolved this conflict in their minds, they will bounce back and forth in their attempts to quit, experiencing multiple relapses. This beginning phase of the mental struggle of recovery is extremely difficult.

> ### The first step toward change is awareness.
> ### The second step is acceptance.
> —*Nathaniel Branden*

Once the recovering person accepts that total abstinence is the *only* answer (social use not being an option), they will reach a point where the mental struggle becomes easier. The minute-by-minute mental struggle fades into the background, and the business of living a new life in recovery becomes more of a focal point.

Let me give you a simple example. About two years into my recovery from drugs and alcohol, I quit smoking. Prior to this period, I had made several failed attempts to stop. Even though I was sick of smoking and was motivated to give up my habit, it was nevertheless very difficult. Finally I decided that no matter what, I was not going to smoke. The next seven to ten days were pure hell. I talked to myself constantly: *Just ten more minutes, I can go ten more minutes.* I was miserable. Every fiber in my body was screaming for nicotine. This went on for about a week or so until the craving faded. I once smoked two packs a day. It has been over thirty years since I quit.

This example should show you that quitting any addiction can be really tough. With alcohol and drug use, the stakes are much higher. With mind-altering drugs, a person needs to know how to quit and also needs help in doing so. It is a much more complicated process than quitting nicotine. There are forces "behind the scenes" working to keep a person addicted. This is a spiritual battle as well as a physical and mental one. God can and will help us to do that which we cannot do on our own—if we will let him.

> *Change does not roll in*
> *on the wheels of inevitability,*
> *but comes through continuous struggle.*
> —*Martin Luther King, Jr.*

Addicts do not see their situation accurately. Their many blind spots need to be revealed in healthy community with those that understand addiction. In most cases, this takes intervention and professional help. No one can beat this problem alone, and addicts need to get to a place where they choose to make serious changes.

Living and enjoying life substance-free is an attainable goal for anyone—regardless of age, length of use, or type of drug. It's never too late to begin the process that brings about dramatic change in a broken life. Recovery is happening every day for numerous men and women. After gaining a bit of clarity, the addict can begin to envision a new life.

Chapter 4
Pick Your Poison

Why do people have "drugs of choice"?

> ### *There's an old man sitting next to me makin' love to his tonic and gin*
> —Billy Joel, *Piano Man*

Often, it's no accident why people may favor one substance over another. Knowing this will help us know more about the person we may be trying to help.

We covered some of the reasons why people take drugs; so let's talk briefly about the three main choices. Knowing these three categories will help us understand why some people seem to have a *drug of choice*.

The three categories of substances are:
- Sedative/Hypnotics
- Stimulants
- Hallucinogens

Almost all psychoactive substances fall into one of these groups. What I mean by *psychoactive* is that the drug influences the mind, or mental process.

Sedative/Hypnotics

This class of drugs will do just what the name implies: sedate the user. These drugs will slow or calm you down. Hence, some are nicknamed "downers." Tense, uptight, or stressed people favor these drugs. Alcohol, Vicodin, oxycodone, methadone, Klonopin, Ativan, Valium, Xanax, heroin, and morphine-based drugs fall into this category—and oh, yes, alcohol *is* a drug. You may think that alcohol isn't a sedative, since it helps people become the life of the party—funny, loud, and with a loss of inhibitions—but that's just the initial effect, which will make the user more talkative and ready to hit the dance floor (one of the reasons alcohol is called "the social lubricant"). As the night goes on, however, these same people will slow down, and may at some point even pass out.

When a person combines opiate pain medications such as Vicodin with alcohol, the risk of an overdose greatly increases. Being aware of such dangers can save a life. Over 50 percent of adults use alcohol, and most do so in moderation. But for an ever-growing percentage, alcohol is causing some devastating problems and addictions—especially when combined with medications.

> *Mother needs something today to calm her down*
> *And though she's not really ill*
> *there's a little yellow pill*
>
> —Rolling Stones, *Mother's Little Helper*

Drugs like Valium, Librium, Ativan, and Xanax are prescribed for people with anxiety or sleep problems. Stressed-out moms raising kids were good candidates for using Valium—hence, it came to be called *mother's little helper*. This was before we knew the consequences of long-term use. As I've mentioned already, these drugs work—and work quite well. That is why some people continue to take them and choose not to quit. Over the years, I took a lot of Valium. This is a tough drug to quit. When prescribed for short periods of time and taken as directed, it can be very beneficial. However, anyone who uses Valium for long periods of time will develop a dependency. When they stop using it, they will go through some form of withdrawal.

Some people take painkillers for physical pain, often prescribed after surgeries or injuries. These drugs also have a high risk for abuse. Why? Because along with killing the pain, they also produce a mild euphoric effect. They can make a person feel good—both physically and mentally. (In a later chapter, I will talk about how a person can take these when necessary, without starting his or her addiction all over again.)

Alcohol is the drug that works for the largest group of people. First of all, you don't need to go to a doctor to get it. And, it is available at most social gatherings, such as weddings and parties. Many people feel a little awkward or shy in a large group setting. Others may be stressed after a long workday and want a drink to relax. Still others may use alcohol merely to dull the pain of unmet needs. You might think of it as the multi-purpose drug, which may be the reason it is used more than all other drugs combined. Alcohol also causes *more harm* than all other drugs combined. Drivers under the influence of alcohol alone kill over 15,000 people a year in the U.S., to say nothing of all the domestic abuse cases in which alcohol plays a role.

Stimulants

These drugs also do what the name implies: they get you up and going. Most Americans drink coffee in the morning to start their day. No big deal. Coffee is tolerated well by most people. This group of users is made up of men and women whose nature or problem may be lack of motivation or who struggle with bouts of depression. Some of the drugs that fall into the stimulant category are at least one hundred times more powerful than the caffeine in a cup of coffee. These drugs have the primary effect of stimulating a person—both physically and mentally. They also have a pleasurable euphoric effect as well. Amphetamines, cocaine, and methamphetamine ("speed")-type drugs are extremely addictive for this reason. Some also have an aphrodisiacal effect—increasing sexual pleasure. These are the drugs that can keep a person awake for days at a time. The most addictive and dangerous drug in this group is methamphetamine. Why? It is extremely potent and extremely effective. Sadly, it is also very destructive. I will discuss the many negative aspects of this drug in chapter 19.

> ## I tried marijuana once. I did not inhale.
> *—William J. Clinton*

Hallucinogens

Marijuana (a mild hallucinogen), hashish, mushrooms, mescaline, LSD, and ecstasy are some of the drugs in this category. These drugs can make a person hallucinate. Depending on which is taken, the effects will be mild and short-term, or very intense, lasting several hours. The most powerful in this group is LSD. What many people do not know is that addiction to this drug is extremely rare. Users will typically try LSD a few times, but most drug users stay away from it. The high, for many, is just too unpredictable. A "bad trip" is often quite scary.

Marijuana, on the other hand, is used by millions of people—both young and old. Some baby boomers started over thirty years ago and are still using it. I often get asked, "Can you become addicted to or dependent on marijuana?" I once heard a guy say, "I've been smoking this for ten years and I'm not hooked yet!" Studies now confirm that approximately ten percent of people who start smoking pot will become dependent on it.

As you may already know, you can now get a license to purchase "medical" marijuana—supposedly for pain control. Any drug, substance, or behavior that produces pleasure has the potential to be repeated. Marijuana ("weed") dependence is mainly psychological. Physical craving or physical withdrawal from this drug is considered mild. Marijuana use, however, has many other side issues that may cause problems for the user, especially the heavy user. Lack of motivation, memory problems, and the tendency to follow up by experimenting with harder drugs are all associated with smoking weed. The drug-using world is run by supply and demand. Those who want to use substances need to purchase them from those who are selling them. Drug dealers rarely, if ever, specialize in only one drug. Many who sell weed will sell other drugs as well. Hence, there is always the temptation to experiment with stronger and more addictive drugs.

> *You know me, I'm your friend*
> *your main boy, thick and thin*
> *I'm your pusherman*
>
> —Curtis Mayfield, *Pusherman*

As for myself, I started with alcohol—orange and cherry vodka. It tasted great! I think it must have been created with kids in mind, kind of like a liquid candy that makes you feel good.

I was thirteen when I first tried alcohol. On weekends, most of the kids my age hung out at a movie theatre. Across the street was a vacant lot where we would sit around and drink. We would find someone to buy what we wanted from the liquor store on the same block. It was summertime in Overland Park, a suburb of Kansas City. I drank it fast— so fast that I puked my guts out. But I loved the way it made me feel.

Shortly after that, I began using speed and other amphetamines. When I was young, I was, and still am today, somewhat reserved and a little awkward in large groups. Alcohol gave me the courage and confidence I lacked when I was with a lot of people. Alco-

> *Alcohol gave me the courage and confidence I lacked.*

hol and amphetamines together not only took away my inhibitions, but even provided me with more confidence. This combination made me seek out groups of people and parties to go to. Later, I discovered co-caine. When I used this drug, it not only felt great to be around others, but I also became a lot "smarter." In fact, I could have answered just about any question a person asked me! This is something most users of cocaine feel—tremendous euphoria and a false sense of omniscience. I was beginning to like what is called *the synergistic effect* of using sev-eral drugs in combination.

For me, it was like a big chemistry experiment—drinking, smoking weed, using coke and, when I got too wound up, taking some Valium to slow down. I used drugs like this for several years, trying to find that just-right combination. Coke, heroin, speed, alcohol, you name it—I used it to excess. I didn't care for the stronger hallucinogens such as LSD. To take LSD, you have to be willing to give up complete control of your mind for several hours, unsure of where your "trip" will take you. Toward the end of my heavy experimentation, right before I went into treatment, I found that I didn't like marijuana either. All it did was make me paranoid. I had become paranoid enough as it was without tak-ing a drug that added to it. By that time, my drug use had robbed me of the ability to feel good, regardless of what I used.

One of the biggest changes in the addiction world over the past few decades is technology—some things that are common today weren't part of the 60s and 70s drug culture. Primarily, I'm talking about the ability to smoke drugs. Back then, I smoked a lot of weed, hash (hashish), and some opium once in a while, but nobody could smoke coke or speed. Today this is possible, and it has changed the whole drug culture. In chapter 6, I will explain how and why.

> *It has become appallingly obvious*
> *that our technology has exceeded our humanity.*
> —*Albert Einstein*

Chapter 5
Houston, We Have a Problem!

How do you know when "use" has turned to "abuse," and "abuse" to addiction?

When someone is dependent on alcohol or drugs, there are signs that can help us know that there really is a problem. Family and friends can look for clues. The challenge for most people is discerning when use and abuse turns into addiction or chemical dependency.* Someone can be a heavy drinker, yet not necessarily addicted to alcohol. But every alcoholic is a heavy drinker. There is no exact way to determine the precise moment that addiction occurs. It's like trying to look at the wind — you can't see it, but you know when it is blowing.

Insidious: *working or spreading harmfully in a subtle or stealthy manner. awaiting a chance to entrap; treacherous. harmful but enticing. Developing so gradually as to be well established before becoming apparent.* —Webster's Dictionary

How does this process happen to someone? For many it begins with a normal curiosity, an experiment. This usually starts in the teen years, but not always. I've known several people who started to drink or use drugs much later in life. There are no hard and fast rules concerning addiction and the age that most people start drinking and using drugs. A wealth of information on this topic can be found on the Internet. According to the

---

*I use the terms *addiction, alcoholism* and *chemical dependency* interchangeably because the words are really saying the same thing. If someone is addicted, they are dependent. Some self-help books will spend a lot of time trying to explain subtle differences between the two terms. I've chosen to use the terms *addict, alcoholic* and *dependent person* to describe people with this disease.

Survey Research Center, part of the Institute for Social Research at the University of Michigan, substance use usually starts in high school (see www.monitoringthefuture.com). Before they graduate, over 80 percent of teens have consumed alcohol and 50 percent have used marijuana.

For some young people, this social or recreational substance use is the beginning of future dependency. Roughly 10 percent of this group will become addicted to alcohol and/or drugs. There is so much going on in the life of an adolescent; it can be very difficult to determine how serious a problem may be. Adolescence is such a critical time for human growth and development, and unfortunately it is also the time when a drug addiction is likely to begin.

Substance Use

For some, the recreational phase or experimentation doesn't last long. For others, it can continue for a long time and yet never become a serious problem. For the user who is going to become dependent, this is *stage one*. The social and recreational use will turn into substance abuse. This applies to all age groups. There are many reasons for the progression. Some people will abuse as a result of of peer pressure, personal problems, or an attempt to cope with physical or sexual abuse. Or, it can be much more simple — the person *just plain likes it*! The beginning stage has very few, if any, signs to detect. It's fun, and it's not yet a problem.

> *My makeup wasn't smeared,*
> *I wasn't disheveled, I behaved politely,*
> *and I never finished off a bottle,*
> *so how could I be alcoholic?*
> —Betty Ford

Substance Abuse

Social users function well, go to work or school, get up on time in the morning, and handle life fairly well. It's a different story for those who move into the abusive phase. This is when you start to see signs of trouble. This person is using more and more often and the negative consequences are beginning to show up in his or her life. Typically, family and friends will see a change in attitude as well. The recreational user is now becoming preoccupied with drinking or getting high. He will start to plan his life around using.

During the abuse phase, it's common to see someone change right in front of your eyes. This phase can last a long time as well, but it doesn't always turn into addiction. Consequences continue to pile up—family problems, work problems, school problems, legal problems, health problems—and this will often be enough to get a person to either quit or cut way back. Unfortunately, this is not the case for those who will become dependent.

> *Sooner or later everyone sits down*
> *to a banquet of consequences.*
> —Robert Louis Stevenson

Addiction

Upon entering the addiction phase, excessive users get progressively worse. Various clues that they are in this stage will make the change obvious to a concerned friend or loved one. The addict now has friends that are also abusers, but they will often become more and more isolated. Some will go to great lengths to over-compensate and cover up their drinking and drug use. When confronted, they will lash out in anger. There is no exact moment when your son, daughter or best friend becomes addicted. It's as if some invisible line gets crossed, and then there's no turning back, no returning to social use. Those days are long gone. I've heard family and friends say it's as if a stranger has moved in.

> *It's like falling in love.*
> *You can't put your finger on the exact time,*
> *you just know it happened.*
>
> —*Dr. Ted Nissen*

There are four things that need to be understood if recovery is to take place in a person's life. Both the abuser and the family need to be clear regarding these elements in order to overcome addiction. This disease is

1. primary,
2. progressive,
3. chronic, and
4. fatal.

1. It's primary.

The addiction is first in order of importance in the person's life. Addiction is at the heart of every user's life and problems. I can remember planning my days around using. If I knew I was going to be gone all day,

I would make sure to have plenty of dope with me and take time to roll some joints and have pills or coke on hand.

2. It's progressive.

As long as the person contin-ues to ignore the fact that their addiction is at the core of their problems, all areas of their life

> *I can remember planning my days around using.*

will get progressively worse. Their physical and mental health may suffer; they may miss work, have trouble raising their family, or experience marital difficulties. Nothing in life will get better until the primary problem is recognized and dealt with. The disease is in its early stages. If left untreated, it continues to get worse. Do not think it will just go away.

Regarding my experience, I began to use more drugs and use them more often. As my tolerance increased, I required stronger substances to get the effect I desired.

3. It's chronic.

This means that the disease will always be with the addicted person. There is no cure for addiction. With the right treatment, it will go into remission, and it will stay in remission as long as the person doesn't start using again. My disease of addiction is in remission. It's not gone; it's just not active. I could reactivate it if I decided to try using again. But I know that choosing to do this would mean that this voracious disease would come back full-force and quickly gain complete control over my life.

> ### Why do I have to stop?
> —*John Belushi*

4. It's fatal.

If left untreated, addiction is fatal—just like many other serious diseases. There are several ways it can take a life. It works on the installment plan, taking a life little by little, with time spent in jails, prisons, institutions, or even causing a person to be homeless or isolated at home. It may take a life quickly, due to a fatal accident, or it can be the cause of poor health. The only hope for people like me is to put the disease into remission and leave it there. This is how to win over addiction.

The truth will set you free. Sometimes the truth is hard to confront, and it can be a lot easier to avoid reality and not face what is really going on with an abuser. We don't want to believe that drugs or alcohol could ever control a family member or a friend. But facing reality and carefully looking for clues can ultimately make all the difference in successfully beating the disease.

Chapter 6
Technology Meets Dope

How has technology changed the world of drugs?

> *Technological progress is like an axe in the hands of a pathological mind.*
> —*Albert Einstein*

Technology is a wonderful thing when applied to products and ideas with socially redeeming values. But when used for the wrong purposes, it can do a lot of harm. In the late 70s and early 80s, technology hit the drug market. People could suddenly smoke drugs such as cocaine and speed. Free-basing was the first attempt to find a way to smoke cocaine. The process was quickly perfected, and soon evolved to what we call crack cocaine. The end result was that a user could turn the powder into chunks that could be put in a pipe and smoked. A similar process works the same way for speed or methamphetamine.

Why is this a big deal? Prior to this new technology, a person could only swallow, snort, or inject powdered drugs such as cocaine, speed, and heroin. If a drug was swallowed, they had to wait for their stomach to break it down and carry it through their bloodstream. Snorting brought on the effect a bit more quickly. IV drug use was a big social taboo—a line most users were not willing to cross—although when they did, the high or rush from the drug was both intense and instantaneous.

Abusers in this group had two things happening at the same time: an intense rush on the spot, as well as the longer-lasting euphoric effect. An IV drug user can immediately taste the drug, smell it, and feel it hit the brain all in a couple of seconds. This experience is very addicting. IV drug use is the "ultimate" in instant gratification. It also carries the highest price tag when it comes to consequences.

Now, new technology has made it possible for users to *smoke* hard drugs and get the same intense rush that IV drug users experience without the *needle freak* stigma attached to it. This has been a big contributing factor in higher addiction rates.

New Technology and Meth

We have all heard about crack cocaine and crystal meth. In the 80s, crack cocaine use was the big story, but then the 90s saw a big surge in meth use. More people became addicted more quickly to meth than ever before. One reason for this switch was the cost. Cocaine was much more expensive and the high didn't last very long. Methamphetamine was much cheaper and the high, which is similar to crack cocaine, lasted for several hours instead of several minutes. I have often heard people say that they became addicted the first time they tried meth—sometimes referred to as the "walk-away drug." Appropriately named, users will often walk away from everything important in their lives for this kind of high. Family, friends, jobs, children, careers— you name it, people have given it all up for this drug.

> *A person can get the same intense rush that IV drug users experience without the "needle freak" stigma attached to it.*

> *In the end it bites like a snake*
> *and poisons like a viper.*
> *Your eyes will see strange sights*
> *and your mind imagine confusing things.*
> —*Proverbs 23:32,33*

One of the reasons for the high rate of crime and gang activity associated with this drug is that people are willing to risk their lives (and yours, too, if you let them) to continue using.

New Technology and Marijuana

Another example of the impact of technology on drug use is in the way marijuana is produced. Over the years, growing high-potency weed has become a real science. With increases in the amount of tetrahydro-cannabinol, or THC (the chemical in the plant that creates the high), today's marijuana is ten to twenty times more powerful than the "grass" that was smoked in the 60s and 70s. Back then, a person could purchase an ounce of pot for ten or twenty dollars, and it was good enough to get you stoned. Today an ounce of high quality/high potency weed can go for several hundred dollars. As I write this, I cringe to think about what future *advances* unbridled technology might bring to the world of pharmaceuticals.

People can now go to a doctor and get a prescription for "medical marijuana" to help with their "pain management." This has become a back-door entrance to legalize weed. There are now hundreds of loctions all across the country that sell pot to those who have prescriptions. The typical client/patient who gets this "script" is a twenty-three-year-old male.

As of this writing, Colorado reports sixty locations that legally sell this drug and hundreds of applications pending—from people who want to open new "boutiques."

We've been discussing how easy it can be for anyone to become addicted to drugs much stronger than marijuana. However, dependence or addiction looks different for different drugs, and people can become dependent on any of them. When I work with offenders in jails or prisons, some talk about getting off drugs, quitting cocaine or speed (the hard drugs), but according to them, pot wasn't a problem. Many would even tell me that they "quit using" a long time ago, but when I asked them about smoking pot, they said "Oh yeah, I still smoke pot," as if it wasn't even a drug. As far as I know, the reason to smoke it is to get stoned. In reality, these people are just switching from one drug to another.

Technology and New Drugs

One last reason for the current drug addiction epidemic is the drug industry itself. Technological advances have enabled drug manufacturers to create drugs that work more efficiently. As these new drugs are brought to market, they seem to find a way into the illicit drug world. OxyContin is one example. This very powerful painkiller has the street nickname *hillbilly heroin*. Why? It works and acts just like heroin. For people with severe chronic pain or a terminal illness, it can keep them comfortable and pain-free. But drug dealers also find ways to get and sell drugs like this one to people who don't need it for medical reasons.

> *One pill makes you larger*
> *and one pill makes you small*
> *and the ones that mother gives you*
> *don't do anything at all.*
> —Jefferson Airplane: *Go Ask Alice*

Chapter 7

Moving On

Making peace with the past.

One of the most difficult things people have to do, addicted or not, is to take responsibility for themselves. Before I was in recovery, I hated the thought of becoming a responsible, mature adult.

I'm not minimizing the tragic or horrible abuse that some addicts have endured throughout their lives. These are *real* issues that require a lot of counseling. Child abuse, assault, rape, emotional abuse, bullying, physical abuse, and trauma can leave scars, leading some to continue the cycle of abuse. Help is available and it's never too late to seek it, and the longer someone waits, the more difficult recovery becomes. But no matter when or how it happens, at some point addicts need to deal with their issues, move forward and take control of their future.

I'll give an example from an experience I had at one of the jails where I worked. Karen, who was in her late twenties, was in jail on a drug charge and had a long history of drug abuse. She was distraught and going through withdrawal. I listened intently as she told me about her family problems, losing her children to social services, and run-ins with the police. This particular county jail, like most, dealt with a transient population. Men and women would come and go all the time, so while it was common to provide initial counseling for an inmate, it was often difficult to schedule follow-up sessions and, consequently, to see any progress. In this situation, I knew I needed to make the most of the time I had.

I tried to offer some hope and encouragement and told her about resources that might help. For most of the hour I spent with her, Karen was in tears. Right before our time was up and the guards came to take her back to her cell, she shared one last thing. In her early teens, at a church camp, an older man, a camp counselor, had raped her. Then to my surprise she said, "I've never told anyone this before." Karen had been carrying this inside of her for half of her life. I was able to see her a few more times and helped her to begin the healing process.

Karen's case was extreme. You can't just tell someone like her, "It's time to grow up." She was carrying around deep-seated, unresolved pain.

The history of most addicts is not as painful as Karen's. For many, drug and alcohol abuse didn't start with a tragedy. I drank and used because it was fun, and I liked the way it made me feel. As time went on, though, I became more drug-dependent. I needed something to blame for my continued use. So, I focused on everything that was wrong in my life, instead of myself. I didn't get along with my Dad. My first marriage (which ended in divorce) was stressful. I had insomnia. I had financial pressures, and my parents wouldn't loan me any more money. I had legal problems. You name it, and I used it as an excuse for my poor choices. Somebody or something was always the scapegoat. I would say, "If you only knew the problems I have, you would understand!" I also had an attitude problem. My rebellious nature and the idea that "no one is going to tell me what to do" kept me stuck for many needless years.

Some parents are even more than willing to jump in and take the blame, convinced that there was something they could have done to prevent the problem. But when my mother would ask me why I used drugs, I'd just tell her the truth: *I don't like the way I feel when I'm straight.*

At some point we all need to become willing to deal honestly with our "stuff." When an addict confronts his own issues, he can start to put things into perspective and make peace with the past and with himself.

This was true even for Karen. She finally realized that the best thing to do was to confront her ugly past. This is a key point in the recovery process. Working through one's junk will bring healing. Somewhere along the way, we all need to say, "That was then, and this is now. I can't change the past no matter how traumatic it may have been, but I can change the future."

This is all part of the process. It is why we need to be patient and trust the recommended course of action. Karen needed physical, mental, emotional and spiritual healing.

> *For I know the plans I have for you,*
> *declares the Lord, plans to prosper you and not to*
> *harm you, plans to give you hope and a future.*
> —*Jeremiah 29:11*
>
> *People can do whatever they want if they*
> *just set their heart to it, and just never give up,*
> *and just go out there and do it.*
> —*Bethany Hamilton, author and surfing champion*

Sometimes people will glibly say that "everything happens for a reason; it's all part of God's will." This is a moronic statement. I believe there are many events throughout our lives and world history that have *absolutely nothing* to do with God's will. There are very real forces of good and evil in the world. I'm confident that one day there will be perfect justice. In spite of all the tragedies of the past, there is still a God who loves us—and He is able to empower us to move forward with confidence.

Time is able to heal many of life's wounds, and this is an important truth to remember in the recovery process. Time, effort, and knowing what to do are the keys to recovery. As concerned friends and family, we really have only one other option — and that is to let the addiction win. Don't let it.

As a parent, spouse, counselor, or good friend, we should be compassionate and empathetic when someone has become drug dependent. Part of our role is to listen and offer encouragement. No matter how unfair or brutal life may have been in the past, the addict must find a way to make peace with the past and move on. The first step in that process is learning to trust someone with their story, just as I trusted my story to the counselors at Valley Hope. Supportive relationships are essential in developing trust, and every dependent person needs to feel accepted to begin to move toward recovery.

In the movie *Bagger Vance*, a war hero returns home and begins using alcohol to try to block out the horrors he witnessed in combat. A young boy confronts him about his drinking and asks the question, *How drunk is drunk enough?*

> "Good question, Hardie. Come over here and take a seat and I'll tell you how drunk is drunk enough. The question on the table is, 'how drunk is drunk enough' and the answer is that it's all a matter of brain cells. Every drink of liquor you take kills a thousand brain cells. But that doesn't much matter because we've got billions more. First the sadness cells die, so you smile real big. Then the quiet cells go, so you just say everything real loud for no reason at all. But that's OK too because the stupid cells go next, so everything you say is real smart. And finally come the memory cells. These are tough sons of bitches to kill."

Karen may never be able to "un-remember" a bad event from her past, but she can choose to accept it and move on, knowing that one day there will be *perfect justice*.

Chapter 8
Inside the Criminal Mind

*Is he an addict with a crime problem
or a criminal with an addiction problem?*

> *Good people do not
> need laws to tell them to act responsibly,
> while bad people
> will find a way around the laws.*
>
> —*Plato*

In my sixteen years working in prisons, counseling men and women incarcerated for virtually every crime you can think of, I've heard hundreds of crime-and-drug stories. What is the connection between crime and drugs? What conclusions can be drawn after digesting all the research and data? Do alcohol and drugs make criminals out of ordinary men and women?

Concerning drug and alcohol addiction, I've concluded that there are two different scenarios or groups.

Group #1

The first group consists of addicts who commit crimes to pay for their habit. Because drug dependency eventually becomes severe, some addicts lose their ability to function on the job. This, in turn, leads to a life of stealing and other petty crimes in order to feed their habit. Such a lifestyle involves drug possession and drug dealing as well. Many addicts and alcoholics will sell drugs on a small scale in order to just get by or to get their own personal drugs for *free*.

Some of the people I have counseled in jail had fairly normal backgrounds before they started using drugs. The story of one such inmate, named Mark, may illustrate how an average young man's life can rapidly deteriorate—as an addiction leads to jail.

> "I was born in Rochester, New York and was raised in a middle-class family. I had a fun childhood and a loving, caring family who would do anything for me. Through middle school, I liked to play baseball, hockey, and video games. I did okay in school. My father was in sales, so we moved around a lot. In high school it was hard to make friends since I was often the new kid and because I was fairly shy. I began hanging out with some older kids who accepted me, and I started skipping classes and partying.
>
> "I met Becky, who introduced me to Ecstasy and shortly after, I began snorting coke. The first time I tried coke was like nothing I had ever experienced before—suddenly I was outgoing, not afraid of anything and I had more friends than ever. For the first time I felt like I was a part of something and I felt cool. People wanted to hang out with me. At first I used only on weekends, but shortly after, this turned into an everyday occurrence.
>
> "Eventually I was using so much I quit school and began selling cocaine. I left my parents' house and went to live with a friend, spending the next five years drinking, smoking, doing coke, and selling drugs. I was out

of control. I *had* to use just to feel okay. I couldn't go anywhere without getting high first.

"I knew something was not right one night at a party when all of a sudden my friend looked at me with alarm and told me that my nose was bleeding. I didn't feel anything. I looked down and my shirt had blood on it. This started happening more often. I decided to quit cocaine and just use other drugs. My twisted reasoning told me that if I wasn't using cocaine, then it was okay.

"By then I was staying at different people's houses. One of the guys I met was using heroin. I decided to try it. At first I snorted the drug, but then I was told that it was way better to shoot it. Right away I was in love with heroin. There was no way I could hold a job or even interview for one. I sold drugs to support my habit.

"At 7:30 a.m. October 11, 2004, the Drug Task Force team woke me up with a warrant for my arrest. I spent the next six months in jail. I still owe $1,800 in restitution. I was charged with four felony counts of sales, which were reduced to one. Today, I'm on probation.

"If I hadn't been using drugs, I would never have sold them, and never would have ended up in 'the system.' I didn't know how sucked in I was until I got sober. Drugs clouded my reasoning to the point that I accepted things I normally would not have been involved with. Now I work hard every day to make sure that I don't get tempted to return to my old lifestyle.

"My story is similar to that of many other addicts.

I want people to know that if you do decide to use heroin, for that brief moment of pleasure, be prepared for a lifetime of pain and suffering. It's been a long hard road. Very quickly I lost everything and everyone who mattered to me. My family doesn't want anything to do with me. Today I struggle with my sobriety. I attend a weekly outpatient program and 12-step group meetings almost every day. Life is completely different being sober. I know that if I do what I am supposed to do, I have a chance to live a normal life again. Maybe someday my family will accept me and I will have a family of my own as well."

—*Mark H.*

The big drug dealers are running a business and some are making a lot of money. Eventually, even they will get caught. I don't know of any large gated-communities where successful drug dealers retire—unless it is a prison complex or a graveyard.

A significant number of those in jail for alcohol or drug problems are from the homeless community. The majority of people in this group have severe and chronic mental health issues.

There are also a large number of people in jail for offenses related to driving while under the influence of drugs or alcohol. I have counseled men and women who felt a great deal of remorse over auto accidents that have caused much harm. Many people in this first group of addicts are in jail or prison directly because of their addiction.

Group #2

Then there are *criminals* with addiction problems. There is a difference here. This group is made up of real criminals. With or without alcohol and drugs, they would be committing crimes. These people have a different mindset from the first group I described*. Only a small percentage of addicts are involved in carjacking, burglary, armed robbery, and sexual assault—those who are were probably criminals to begin with.

Taking Responsibility

No matter if a person is from Group #1 or Group #2, it is important for them to *take responsibility for their crimes* and not to blame the drugs themselves.

There seems to be a trend lately in which movie stars, comedians, and politicians caught in criminal behavior, or sometimes merely using slanderous speech, opt to check into rehab. Why? Very often, they are not willing to take responsibility for their behavior. *I'll blame this on my alcohol or drug problem.* They may not need rehab at all, but rather just need to own up to the fact that they displayed poor behavior.

There is a lot of confusion when it comes to understanding crime and users. Why bring this up? I've sat in many court rooms and have been called to testify concerning these matters. Just because a criminal might be a user doesn't mean that *his addiction* is causing him to live a life of crime. The reality is that many criminals do not pay for their crimes and learn from them, because the blame is placed on the drugs, not the user. I don't believe drug dependency should be used as a defense.

Do we need more treatment for offenders with substance abuse issues? Of course! Freedom from drugs would help all offenders to make

*In the book, Inside the Criminal Mind, author Stanton Samenow explores this group in great detail.

better choices. But to lump all criminals and drug-dependent men and women together is a mistake. As a friend or family member who is trying to help an addict, it is very important that you have a good working knowledge of the dynamics of crime and drugs. Don't allow the offender to manipulate the reality of the situation. When we hear a parade of attorneys talking about their clients' substance abuse problems being the cause of their criminal behavior, we should all be concerned, as this never helps the user recover.

This is a high-priced version of the blame game. When people decide they need to blame someone or something, two things

> *Don't allow the offender to manipulate the reality of the situation.*

happen. First, the criminal believes that their behavior is excusable because the fault lies somewhere else; they had *little or no control* over the event. Secondly, and even worse, is the belief that the perpetrator is also a victim. Now we have two victims and no one taking responsibility.

Let me illustrate this by telling another story. A few years ago there was a high-speed chase in town at three o'clock in the afternoon, at a time when parents were picking their children up from school. The police were in the process of pulling a man over for speeding when he took off again. It was later determined that this man was high on drugs and also severely intoxicated. The chase ended as the man broadsided a car carrying a mother and her two small children. Both children were killed and the mother was paralyzed from the neck down.

As the jail chaplain, I was asked to counsel this man who caused the accident. He remorsefully told me that he was so very sorry for the harm he caused this family. Then he added something I'll never forget. He said that it wasn't his fault. *If the police wouldn't have been chasing him, the whole thing could have been avoided.*

After a while, criminals actually come to believe such thinking. The addict/criminal reasons, *If I really think that someone or something other than myself is the cause of my problem, then I'm not responsible; someone else is.*

> ### *When you blame others,*
> ### *you give up your power to change.*
> —*Robert Anthony*

Family members or friends witnessing this cycle of thinking will become extremely frustrated. They are able to see that the addict has a very inaccurate view of himself, but often they're not able to make the perpetrator see reality. At this point, those in supportive roles will need to be patient.

It is important to be reminded not to give up! Even when relationships become strained, people can still change. A treatment center may be the catalyst for the addict to see their problem for what it actually is, as they will be hearing the truth from objective parties. Surprisingly, family and friends may find that a treatment center or resource is a setting where their loved one can be humbled, and heed correction and counsel that they would not hear from someone close to them. It can make all the difference and put an end to the blame game.

Even if you have to detach and not communicate with the person, never forget that you can still pray. Pray that an event or circumstances will happen which will allow him or her to see the light. People often look back to see how God has intervened in a life—usually in a way that we never would have imagined.

Part 1 Overview:
Key Points to Remember

- **Quitting and recovery are two separate issues:**
  - *quitting simply means to stop all use of alcohol and drugs;*
  - *recovery is a process that takes time to restore and repair all the damage that was done during active addiction;*
  - *recovery has three components: physical, mental and spiritual.*

- **People use substances to increase pleasure and decrease pain.**

- **No one sets out to purposefully become an alcoholic or drug addict.**

- **Quitting is not an easy thing to do:**
  - *physical withdrawal can be difficult;*
  - *mental struggle is a very tough battle.*

- **Three categories of drugs are**
  - *sedative/hypnotics*
  - *stimulants*
  - *hallucinogens*

- **Progression of addiction:**
  - *use (recreational/experimental);*
  - *abuse (the addict still functions fairly well, but starts to see consequences);*
  - *addiction (cannot control use in spite of consequences).*

- **Four aspects of addiction:**
  - *it's primary (first in order of importance in the person's life);*
  - *it's progressive (gets worse over time);*
  - *it's chronic (lasts forever);*
  - *it's fatal.*

- **Technology has made it possible to become addicted much faster than before:**
  - *the ability to smoke certain drugs has increased their popularity;*
  - *potency of marijuana has dramatically increased since the 70s;*
  - *powerful prescription drugs are finding their way to the illegal drug market.*

- **Friends and family need to have empathy but also help the addict to move past the blame, take responsibility and concentrate on a solution.**

- **When addicted criminals blame someone else two things happen:**
  - *they believe their actions are excusable;*
  - *they believe they are also a victim.*

It's a Family Affair

Chapter 9

None of Your Business

Should you intervene or not?

> ### *I need someone to tell me*
> ### *which way I oughta go.*
> —JJ Cale, *Dead End Road*
>
> ### *Your word is a lamp to my feet*
> ### *and a light for my path.*
> —Psalm 119: 105

One of the myths I believed for a long time was that my substance use was my problem, and my problem alone. *Leave me alone*. If I wanted advice, I'd ask for it. But nothing was further from the truth. In the poker game "Texas Hold 'Em," players will occasionally push their chips forward and say, "I'm all in." Whether we like it or not, addiction affects the entire family. We're "all in" and there is no option to *not play*. This is a problem that directly impacts everyone in the family. It affects some family members more than others, but no one gets to pass.

The scenario plays out differently depending on the relationships involved. Whether you are a spouse, mother, brother, uncle, or any other relation, there will be either a direct effect or some form of spillover to other members of the family. These problems are usually discussed among family members, and as a result, others start to share the stress and burdens. This happens more with addiction than with many other problems. There are several reasons for this. One is obvious—we care about and love the people closest to us and we sometimes fear that our loved one will destroy himself. Another reason is the tremendous amount of shame and guilt that seems to be associated with alcoholism and addiction. Many people look at addiction as a mental health problem, which has its own stigma.

The Role of the Family

Because addiction never goes away, we often see a loved one with this problem relapse back to old behaviors. It is not unusual for this to happen several times before we see longer periods of abstinence and, ultimately, complete abstinence. When family and friends get their hopes up again and again, only to be repeatedly disappointed, it is extremely frustrating for them. Fortunately, there are ways to minimize the heartache.

First, do not try to fix the situation on your own. Often, family members will blame themselves and will try to solve the problem alone. But family members are too close to the problem and sometimes too emotional to see things objectively, so getting some wise counsel will pay real dividends. Help doesn't always have to be professional (meaning that one has to pay for the advice) or expensive. Many

> *Do not try to fix the situation on your own.*

people know of others dealing with the same issues who can provide support and resources. Many churches now offer counseling for substance abuse and have staff who are trained for this ministry.

Al-Anon, (a support group just for family and friends of substance abusers and alcoholics) is a free resource and worth checking out. I also recommend attending a few "open AA" meetings. A friend or family member can learn a great deal about addictive thinking from listening to those in recovery tell their stories. Anyone can attend an open AA meeting. Just sit and listen.

> ### Plans fail for lack of counsel,
> ### but with many advisers they succeed.
> *—Proverbs 15:22*

There are also many private counselors who invoice on a sliding scale. In addition, city and county governments usually have programs that are available at no cost. Addiction is a problem that requires using various means to bring about lasting change. Having these issues sorted out by an objective third party is well worth the time and effort. (In the Appendix I've listed resources for you to consider.)

Often, family members will wait a long time, thinking that things will work out on their own. There is too much at stake to take this approach. Sometimes doing the right thing will make you feel horrible. You can know that the positive results and good feelings will come much later. It has been said that there are three ways to deal with a problem—to do the right thing, the wrong thing, or nothing. The worst choice is to do nothing.

Intervention

We've all done interventions at various times in our lives, whether we realize it or not. An *The worst choice is to do nothing.*

intervention can be anything from telling a child to be careful on their bike and be sure to watch for cars, to asking someone to clean up their desk or office at work. For the addict, intervention will make all the difference.

We now see PSAs (Public Service Announcements) on television that tell us, *Friends don't let friends drive drunk.* If you've ever suggested to someone that they were too drunk to drive, you know how awkward it can be. One of the rules I try to use for myself is this: If it's the right thing to do, then I want to be sure to do it, and if it's the wrong thing to do, I want to be sure to avoid it. This is not always easy to put into practice. Nonetheless, it is important, especially concerning the life of someone who may have a substance-use problem. Most likely, you will make mistakes from time to time. Family members can expect to go through great pain and long days of frustration, feeling helpless at times. To this day, I don't know all that I put my family through.

> "Joe's years with drug problems were very sad. It was hard watching him tear down his body. I was afraid he would have a wreck and hurt himself or others. I was afraid he would get arrested and end up in jail.
>
> "I had talked to Joe about getting help. He said he wasn't interested. He said, 'I don't want to go somewhere and have people come and visit and look at me like some kind of freak.' I should have talked to him and explained that it wouldn't be that way, but I really didn't know how it would be. His Dad wanted him to go somewhere for help long before he went. We didn't agree . . . should I make him go? This went on for several years."
>
> —*Gladys Herzanek*

When it comes to intervention, there are more than a few options available. An intervention can sometimes be quick, easy, and free, or it can be much more complicated. Depending on the circumstances, it may be just a brief conversation that has a positive outcome. How long and how much a person has been using will affect the success of an intervention. Sometimes the solution is to pick up the phone and dial 911.

One afternoon during the time that my teenage son, Jake, was abusing drugs, I called 911. I knew the situation was out of control and severe enough that another party needed to intervene. I was too close emotionally and knew it wasn't healthy for me to try to handle his anger toward me.

The police arrived and spoke with both of us, explaining that they didn't have any place to take him, and we should both calm down. The police had been gone only about ten minutes when Jake started trash-talking to me again. As I sat in the living room, he looked down at me from the landing above and proceeded to tell me that he could do whatever he wanted, and there was nothing I could do about it. *Even the cops can't do anything.* That was when I picked up the phone and called 911 for the second time. This time the police told Jake to grab a few things, and they'd take him to one of his friend's homes to spend the night.

Friends and family should remember to never let arguments become physical. Looking back on that day, I'm thankful that I didn't try to handle it alone. It was just *one of those days.*

> ". . . Things between me and my dad were absolutely horrible. Maybe it was me that was driving him crazy, but he *was* crazy. For weeks my dad had been sleeping sitting up in a chair, with a neck injury from a motorcycle accident and was on all types of medication. All I knew was my dad was being a jerk because he felt horrible. So we got into it and were yelling and screaming. He was mad at me, and my point throughout the argument was, 'what are you gonna do about it?' My dad at this point came up with the great idea of calling the cops.

> "Sure enough the cops came. I saw them from my window, climbed out on the roof and jumped down from the second story and talked to them before my dad ... This was about the peak of me and my dad getting into it."
>
> —*Jake Herzanek*

When beginning the process of intervention, a conversation is a good place to start, but it may be perceived as confrontation, something most of us try to avoid. We may ask someone else to have that conversation with the person we're concerned about. But there will be awkward moments no matter which option you choose. To start the process, you may choose to further analyze your family situation. Reading this book is a great start, and you may find the need to send it as a gift to someone in need. If these first, less-invasive attempts appear to have little or no effect, you then may want to consider seeking professional intervention help.

Professional intervention doesn't necessarily have to look like what you may have seen on the A&E channel or other similar shows on TV, when a large group of family and friends confront and surprise the addict or alcoholic. There are times when this approach can be very effective, but there are other, lesser-known strategies that can work as well. Often professionals can do an intervention over the phone with the person that needs help. If you are considering an option like this, please do your homework. Get references, compare them, and compare costs. Prices can vary a great deal and so can effectiveness. The goal is to get the person to see the light and begin recovery.

My intervention was simple: I was given an ultimatum. One of the reasons it worked as well as it did was its timing. When my parents said to me that I either could "get treatment or get out," it was a very low point in my life and my options were running out, as I had no other place to run but to family. I was living in my parents' home at the time. Over the years, I would go from having plenty of money to no money at all. During the no money times, they would reluctantly let me move back in. My memory of this intervention/conversation is still vague to me today. I was so hung over, strung out, and worn out at the time.

> "One evening Joe's dad found some drugs, and he flushed them down the toilet. When Joe found out what his dad did, he was mad as a hornet. Joe confessed he was in big trouble now, and might even be killed, as he was supposed to deliver the drugs to someone. I think there was a lot of money involved. Joe was so high he fell off the stool he was sitting on.
>
> "The next morning when Joe got up, I said I wanted to talk to him. I finally said, 'Joe, I cannot watch you killing yourself anymore. I cannot give you any more money, and you can't live here any more. You have a daughter who I'm sure wants you to be there for her as she grows up . . . if you want help I'll get help for you. It's up to you. But if you choose to continue your life as it is, I don't even want you to come around, 'cause I don't want to see you like you are.' Looking back, I really didn't know what would happen. I just prayed he'd make the right decision. . . . He did, thank God."
>
> —*Gladys Herzanek*

Keep Hope Alive

Some of you who are reading this book are worn out. You've already done all of these things—maybe more than once. You've seen brief periods when things were going well, things appeared to be working and life seemed to have turned a corner—only to come to a screeching halt, causing hurt and disappointment again and again. So what now? When do you give up hope?

> *Hope allows us to keep going*
> *when circumstances are dire*
> *and there does not appear to be*
> *any opportunity of turning the tide.*
>
> *Hope is that little crack in the curtain*
> *that allows a ray of light to shine through.*
> *Hope means believing in a possibility,*
> *even if we only have a scant sliver of faith.*
>
> —*Ned Wicker/Addiction Chaplain*

The time to completely give up hope should never come. There is always hope. Hope, faith and prayer are powerful forces to hold onto. Continuing to be optimistic, regardless of how things appear, is the best outlook to have. Instead of completely giving up, ask yourself, *When do I stop my well-intentioned efforts? When do I step back and quit trying to control this person?* In some situations, there may come a time when you must pull back, and I mean pull back completely. This is difficult; but when you know it's the right thing to do, you have to do it.

> *Do you love your child enough*
> *to let him be mad at you?*
>
> —*Don Williams*
> *Clear Brook Lodge, Shickshinny, PA*

Tough Love

Over the years, I have seen families struggle to come to terms with this hands-off approach. Remember this: Just because you have to step away does not mean that you stop loving and showing empathy for the person. Empathy is better when it is mixed with a little tough love. The consequences that come down on someone who is abusing alcohol and drugs may be their best teacher. If you've confronted the person you are concerned about a few times to no avail, and professionals are saying you need to let go, then you should listen. Others can look at the situation with objectivity. Allowing your loved one's utilities to be turned off, or forcing them

> *Let your loved one know that you care about them, but stand your ground.*

to sleep in the car (or jail) for a few nights, can often work wonders. Let your loved one know that you care about them, but stand your ground.

Every situation calls for discernment and a good understanding of the circumstances. There is, however, a time when intervention is crucial. In the case of someone who is going to harm himself or others, you need to turn the whole thing over to the correct authority. In reality, there are times when even you or the professionals cannot stop a user from harming himself or others. But these situations are extreme and rare. I'm not saying that we should take threats lightly, but once you've done all you can do, it's out of your hands. A large number of substance abusers will eventually make changes. To hope means that you believe the user in need of help will be on the road to recovery, sooner or later.

> *Family members rarely, if ever, cause the problem.*
> *They can't control it or cure it.*
> —*The Three C's*

When actively using, the addict needs to see that he is powerless to control his use. At some point, family and friends need to understand that they also are powerless to make someone think the right thoughts and do the right things. However, being aware of some helpful ways to intervene can bring about peace of mind. To simply pray and wait is difficult. It feels as if you are doing nothing when you should be doing something. But don't give up hope, and know that when you are waiting, praying and being patient you *are* doing something.

Let me give you one last word on intervention. Intervention by a family member, friend, or employer is the way that most people get into treatment. When I use the word treatment, I do not always mean a 28-day program where a person is required to leave home. Treatment can be different for different people. What I am referring to is seeking help, getting counseling, going to groups, outpatient treatment or attending 12-step meetings. If an addict thinks that he can use just willpower to stop, it is not going to work. Some people can quit for a time on their own, but no one can *recover* all alone.

> *Intervention by a family member, friend, or employer is the way that most people people get into treatment.*

It's very rare for someone to just decide on their own that they need to enter a recovery program, or even to admit to their substance-abuse problem. As a friend or family member, you may be the one to initially make the calls to a few treatment centers. A good place to start is to go online to **www.naatp.org** (National Association of Addiction Treatment Providers). This is listed in the Resources section in the back of the book. Once you find a resource you are interested in, you can speak with trained professionals who will suggest some strategies for you and provide you with names of people in your community who are equipped to help.

There are also a growing number of faith-based Christian treatment centers available. One of the objectives of experiencing rehab is to educate the client about the destructive behavior he is inflicting on himself. This is the start of both physical and spiritual recovery.

If you keep "asking and seeking" you will find that there are many resources and people who are happy to help.

Chapter 10

Siblings: The Forgotten Ones

How siblings get hurt.

The Parable of the Prodigal Son

*While he was still a long way off,
his father saw him coming.
Filled with compassion
the father ran to the son,
threw his arms around him and said,
"Welcome home."
His son had come to his senses.
Let's have a party!*

*His brother refused to come to the party
even after his father pleaded with him
to join them.
"I've stayed here all these years
and never caused a problem.
No one ever had a party for me,"
said the brother.*

—*paraphrased from the Gospel of Luke*

Siblings often find themselves caught in the middle of the recovery process. In the story of the prodigal son, a father waits and watches expectantly for the return of his wayward child. The boy left home and not only squandered his inheritance, but also wasted a big chunk of his life. But there is so much more to the story. As we take a closer look at the entire family, we see that "the rest of the story" can apply to families and siblings today who are struggling with addiction or the early stages of recovery.

> ### If we could sell our experiences
> ### for what they cost us,
> ### we'd all be millionaires.
>
> —*Abigail Van Buren*

I know from firsthand experience how siblings can suffer. During my addiction, I was blind to how my actions were affecting my brother and two sisters. Actually, the entire family did not understand what was happening. Even now, more than thirty years later, some members of my family remain bitter, and we have never been able to resolve those hard feelings.

There's only so much time in any given day and when there is one high-maintenance family member, often other children are neglected. Parents have a limited

> *I was blind to how my actions were affecting my brother and two sisters.*

amount of energy, and then they reach a point of exhaustion. In my case, which again is not unique, I received more than my share of attention. I, like many other addicts, was a very needy person. My life was one crisis after another. There were many occasions when I needed money.

I drained my parents of their finances as well as their time and energy. Who suffered? At the time, it was far from obvious, but as I look back it is clear that my brother and sisters—basically good, low-maintenance kids—were the innocent victims. Mom and Dad spent a lot of their parenting energy either helping me with a problem or worried about what I might do next; they were even afraid to answer the phone. They couldn't be in two places at once, physically or mentally. As a result, my siblings did not receive nearly the amount of attention they deserved. My parents missed their school programs and sports games because of my problems, and holidays were often ruined. Much of the focus was on *Joe,* and I was messing up my life while my brother and sisters were left striving to do the right thing and gain my parents' approval and attention.

> ### The years teach much which the days never knew.
> —*Ralph Waldo Emerson*

To make matters worse, my parents' attention continued to be focused on me for a long time into my recovery. My siblings had to hear over and over, *Isn't it great that Joe's quit using drugs? How wonderful that Joe is clean and sober. Joe has been drug-free for a year now—let's celebrate!* These sort of comments continued, even after everything should have been back to normal. Talk about rubbing psychological salt in a wound; my brother and sisters must have been ready to puke. At that time, none of us had a clue how this would ultimately affect our future relationships.

It was only after years of recovery and study on this topic that this realization came to me. Because of this disease's slow progression, few families are aware of the effect addiction has on the family as a whole. Few addicts think of making amends toward those who did not appear to be directly affected.

When I entered treatment many years ago, there was not much emphasis placed on the importance of family in the recovery process. Today, this is a key component in most treatment programs. Parents and siblings are strongly encouraged to be part of the process. Some centers will even offer what is called Family Week. This is a time for those who have been negatively affected to become involved in the recovery process. Many times family members will refuse to get involved: "He/she had the problem, not me. And now you are asking *me* to get counseling? You must be crazy." Nonetheless, I strongly suggest that family members attend some meetings—if for no other reason than to vent frustration. It will be worth it.

Addiction is treacherous for the whole family. Over time, relationships can become a tangled web. Feelings get hurt and bitterness creeps in, almost unnoticed. Strife begins to build, and after a while no one remembers why. But life is too short to waste years like this. Miracles can happen when a professional helps untangle the mess.

One family situation in particular stands out to me. While I was working in the county jail, I came to know a young man named Tommy. I spent many hours trying to help him over a span of about eight years. Though his story may sound uncommon, I'm sure it happens more often than we realize. During my years working as a counselor in jails and prisons, I saw Tommy often. He was what we called a "frequent flyer." I met with him in county jails, prisons, halfway houses, and even at his apartment—although those types of meetings were rare, as he couldn't keep a residence for very long.

One of the reasons I invested my time and energy in Tommy was that he was such a likeable guy, with high energy, a great smile, and an upbeat personality. I believed Tommy had a lot of potential. But in addition to his alcohol problem, he was also a heavy cocaine user.

I continued to get to know him better, and even became acquainted with his mother as well. She lived in a very modest retirement home, which was all she could afford. Often when Tommy was out of jail, he found it necessary to sneak into her apartment at night so he would have a place to sleep. This was a strict *no-no*. The retirement home did not want relatives living with Mom or Dad. Tommy was forty-nine years old and had siblings—siblings that didn't get along with him at all.

Over the previous few decades, Tommy had drained his parents dry. His alcohol, drug, and criminal behavior had cost his parents about a half million dollars. Bailing him out of jail, paying for attorneys, putting money into his account while in jail and prison, setting him up in an apartment when he was released—it all added up. For some families this may not be a big burden, but for Tommy's it was their life savings. His brothers and sister watched the whole thing happen. Finally, they attempted to step in—to insist that their mother stop rescuing him. (This was after his father had passed away.) His mother did stop, of course, when she ran completely out of money.

The story doesn't end here. Tommy did finally get into recovery. He slowly began to heal, and communication with his siblings improved. And now, they no longer dread holidays. He told me that recovery has been both challenging as well as exciting. Real forgiveness is happening within the family. Most importantly, trust is being rebuilt and his family is starting to recover as well.

Time has yet to heal some of the wounds in my family. The impact of my addiction and recovery has left deep scars, and damaged relationships among my immediate family that we are still attempting to understand and mend. Despite our attempts to keep things simple, life can sometimes become very complicated. Over the years, my siblings have married. Bitterness and unresolved strife have colored relationships not only among my siblings, but among our spouses and children as well. Recovery and the process of making amends to those who were hurt takes a while. *Sometimes these differences may never be resolved.*

Quitting, as wonderful as that may be, is not the same as recovering. Recovery means taking responsibility for the broken relationships that occurred when the addict was using. Repairing broken relationships is critical to the process of recovery. With patience and time, progress can be made.

Chapter 11
What's Going On?

Is addiction a disease or a moral failing?

Is addiction a disease? Webster's Dictionary defines disease as: 1) a condition of the living animal or plant body or of one of its parts that impairs normal functioning and is typically manifested by distinguishing signs and symptoms; or 2) a harmful development.

Alcohol or drug addiction satisfies both definitions. It is, in fact, a brain disease. This disease has its own set of diagnosable symptoms that can be measured and treated. At the same time, it is also a spiritual disease. So how does knowing this help you? To the person with the addiction, it helps them to understand what is happening to their body, both mentally and physically. There is a battle going on for the mind — a tug-of-war, you might say. To family members and friends, there is some relief in knowing that their loved one is ill (both physically and spiritually) and not necessarily insane. To hospitals and treatment centers, it means that they can treat the disease and that insurance companies can help cover the cost of treatment.

> *I do not understand what I do.*
> *For what I want to do I do not do,*
> *but what I hate I do.*
>
> —The Apostle Paul speaking to the church in Rome
> Romans 7:15

Perhaps, though, the bigger question is, *How does someone become addicted?* If we can find the cause, maybe we can find a solution. This is a logical question with a not-so-easy answer. First, we must understand the background and history of the addict.

Nature vs. Nurture

Nature looks at things such as genetic makeup; so, *is addiction passed down through the family like many other diseases?* An overwhelming body of evidence says yes—there definitely is a genetic component or link. However, scientists and researchers can't put a sample of the disease under a microscope and analyze it to prove that a link exists. There is also a problem when trying to predict which offspring or family member will develop the disease. This is kind of like a lawyer who builds a large case solely on mountains of circumstantial evidence. And there are many exceptions, too: some people who seem to have no genetic link at all develop the disease, and vice versa.

When we speak of *nurture,* we are referring to environment— where, why, when, and how a person begins and lives out their life. The focus is on factors such as neighborhood, social status, parenting skills, peer group, education, and role models—all of which can play a powerful role in a young person's life. Then again, often children who have grown up in the same home and in the same environment later take drastically different directions in life. This nurture issue can work both ways. The honest truth is that kids from very bad environments and kids from the best homes may both find themselves with addictions. Are the odds stacked against those from less than desirable family backgrounds? I'm sure that they are.

Tragically, some children are raised in abusive homes. I have seen a disproportionate number of addiction cases that involve abuse. Many alcohol- or drug-dependent men and women are carrying a lot of baggage around and are looking for ways to cope with their profound pain.

But not everyone dealing with drug and alcohol abuse has experienced a severe tragedy or can claim a genetic predisposition. There are also those who simply like to drink, drug, and party. No baggage, no broken homes, no abuse. They just like the way they feel when they get high.

This was true in my case. I enjoyed the way I felt when I used drugs. I used for the simple reason that it was fun. Sure, I didn't have a perfect childhood, and my parents could have done a few things differently. But if I'm really honest, I think that I just wanted to be one of the "cool kids," which in my mind meant drinking and getting high. My former wife will attest to the fact that I wanted to portray a certain image. My adolescent years lasted a long time.

There are also those who simply like to drink, drug, and party.
No baggage,
no broken homes,
no abuse.

My nature and nurture were not all that bad. I don't recall any relatives with substance-abuse problems. Neither of my parents ever had more than an occasional drink. In fact, I don't recall ever seeing either one of them drunk. I'm sure if you look long and hard enough, you can find someone in every family who drinks too much. But in my case, if there was a genetic link, it wasn't obvious. No one in my family—mother, father, brother, sisters, aunts, uncles or grandparents—had this disease.

Can addiction be considered a moral failing? Talk about a *hot potato*. In our postmodern and enlightened society, morality is often viewed as closed-mindedness. We speak in terms of tolerance—*what is right for you may not be right for me*. Whose morals are we to use as the standard? Let's look at the word *morals* for a moment. The dictionary defines it as "principles of right and wrong." It mentions character and virtue. Regarding what is right and wrong, whose definition do we accept?

Most everyone would acknowledge that there are some universal absolutes that are generally accepted by a civilized society. For example, it is morally wrong to harm others without cause or for selfish reasons. Are addicts and alcoholics able to distinguish right from wrong? Have they lost touch with reality? Often it takes someone sober to point out the moral dilemmas that this person has caused for the family. For abusers, the drug has controlled them for so long that they often feel there is no other choice than to keep using. The craving has overtaken their ability to fully reason or think rationally.

> ### A man has free choice
> ### to the extent that he is rational.
> —*Saint Thomas Aquinas*

My good friend Michael Connelly, from the Odyssey Training Center in Denver, Colorado, talks about how addiction creates *limited choice*. By *limited* Michael is referring to the ability to resist *just so much* craving or pressure. At some point, the dependent person caves in to the stress. His emotions and cravings overwhelm his decision-making process. There is a limited amount of control exercised. I like this way of explaining it. Looking back again at my own active addiction, I see some parallels. Part of me knew that my heavy substance use was wrong. At times, I felt bad or guilty about the way I was living. But as my addiction progressed and my condition worsened, it became more and more difficult to think clearly, and I didn't experience those guilty feelings as often.

Even from a Christian or biblical perspective some of these topics do not have clear-cut answers. The bible does not condemn drinking alcohol. It does condemn getting drunk and it warns of the potential for abuse.

Recently I watched a news story about a local man who robbed a hospital pharmacy. He came in with a gun, but did not demand money. He knew exactly what he wanted—a very potent painkiller. The pharmacist said that addicts reach a point where they are willing to do anything, even risk their lives for the drug. Did this guy know it was morally wrong to rob someone at gunpoint, to risk killing another person to get his drugs? What was he thinking? For the addict—the person with the malfunctioning brain—his craving of the drug had overwhelmed his thoughts. His addiction was telling him that *his own life* was at stake—that if he didn't get the drugs he needed, he was going to die. To him it was a matter of life or death.

To someone watching the news report, his actions were obviously wrong. This was a *moral failing,* visible to everyone except the addict committing the crime. Once addiction has complete control of the person, the craving can far outweigh the decision-making process and the most unthinkable act becomes rationalized.

In the beginning stages of addiction, some feelings of guilt or shame just might be a good thing. Once someone moves into full-blown dependency, their choices become more and more limited as they try to satisfy their need for drugs. If not for the intervention of my family, I could have eventually become this drug thief myself.

Disease or Moral Failing?

So back to our original question: *Is addiction a disease or a moral failing?* I would have to say that it is both. For me, in the beginning stages, I knew what I was doing was wrong, but the pleasure that the drugs and alcohol produced won over my moral beliefs. After several years of living like this, my addiction brought me to the *limited choice*, or disease level. You could say that a person starts out flirting with danger (a moral failing), and ends up totally consumed by the disease of addiction.

> ### *Drugs are a bet with your mind.*
> —*Jim Morrison*

Chapter 12

I Drink Alone

Why is isolation a bad sign?

When I set out to write this book, I didn't plan to address every aspect of addiction and recovery. Some topics just seem to stand out in my mind more than others. Isolation is one of them. For many, isolation is one of the end results of addiction. What was once a fun and sociable part of life turns into quite the opposite experience. In the fun stage of alcohol or drug use, we often like to be around others—that is, others who like to get high. Substance use often begins with laughter, parties, and hanging out with a group of people. Some people stay in this stage of use, control their drinking, and go on to lead a responsible life. Others, like me, continue to use more and more.

> ### Isolation is the sum total of wretchedness to a man.
> —*Thomas Carlyle*

Drinking Alone
One of the signs of addiction is that the person starts getting high alone. Drinking or using *before* going out partying is part of the addiction process—as is getting high at any time of the day or night. Drinking, taking pills, or smoking dope first thing in the morning may become the norm. Why is this? The drug has now become the primary focus of their life.

At this stage, many addicts will become suspicious and paranoid. Straight people (nonusers) are more difficult for the addict to communicate with. They are potential roadblocks to the person's ability to use. When I reached this point of dependency, I could count my remaining friends on one hand. And most were all users, just like me.

Once the addiction becomes primary, a dependent person's life is preoccupied with using. He spends valuable time and energy planning his day, to make sure he will be able to have access to his needed amount of drugs or alcohol. Substance use has overcome the person's life and it is nearly impossible to hide it. I can remember having tinted glasses made because I didn't want people to see my eyes.

> "Some things that happened I don't remember. I guess I blocked them out, stuff like he was supposed to come for weekends and he wouldn't show. [My mom told me] I would cry and cry... I don't remember that."
>
> —*Jami, my daughter*

Covering Up

Virtually everything in the person's life can become secondary — friendships, family relationships, children, sex, jobs, personal hygene, eating — you name it. At first the person may go out of their way to overcompensate. When they realize that this main focus of their lives is threatening other areas, in an attempt to *have it all,* they may try to maintain a perfect image to prove to those close to them that they don't have a problem. The addict may stay late at work, have people over to dinner, keep a perfectly clean house, and in general try to portray an ideal image. At the same time, they are secretly trying to manage their addiction in isolation. This is referred to as "high functioning."

As the addiction progresses, trying to prove that they are normal becomes more and more difficult, and eventually the addiction completely takes over. This explains why an addicted parent may eventually be forced to give up their child to a relative or social services. People who have lived through this staggering experience know that it's not about love—these parents do love their spouses, family, and children—it's about addiction. The addiction takes hold and consumes their very lives. This is very difficult for any family member or friend to understand, unless they have personally been through it.

This is the point I had reached when I walked out on my wife and seven-year-old daughter. Addiction had completely overtaken my life.

> "My dad was a great dad. He loved me and my mom very much. He wasn't your typical 'run-out-on-your-family' kind of dad. I will never forget the day he left, though.
>
> "He sat me and mom on the couch in our house in Lenexa, and he told me to go get some Kleenex. He told us how much he loved us, and that he just couldn't live with us anymore. It still makes me cry today when I think of it. That house is where I started kindergarten. After that, my mother says she would have to come find me when the school would call because I would start to walk to school and never go; I just sat by the railroad tracks.... She started to take me to school."
>
> —*Jami*

Our society seems to believe that it is far worse for a *mother* to leave her family, but in reality the situation is devastating either way. To add a note of hope, today Jami and my former wife are very close to me, my current wife, Judy, and our two children (Jake and Jess). Our relation-ships today are a tribute to the fact that dramatic changes are possible.

When to Intervene

When addiction overtakes a person's life, and *fun* has become a dis-tant memory, *this is a good time for an effective intervention*. When a user starts to lose things in their life that they truly used to care about, they may not know how to turn things around. They might feel help-less, and stop believing it is possible to make life matter again. In this situation, the best thing for the dependent person is to talk to someone who has *been there*. They will often say that they don't want treatment. I've heard it said that "Treatment won't work unless a person wants it." Well, when I got to this point, *I didn't want it,* but I was forced to go.

My life was in shambles. Nothing was working, and all I could think to do was to keep using. The reality of what I had become was too much for me to bear. Life seemed both hopeless and meaningless. Everything revolved around staying under the influence — anything that kept me from *thinking*. It was at this point that my family stepped in. Looking back, I realize now that their intervention saved my life. I had left my wife and child and was isolating myself — living in my parent's basement. They recognized the danger and offered me the help I needed. Treatment was the best thing that ever happened to me. I was able to claim my life back, and no longer live in shame and isolation.

Chapter 13
Raising Kids in the Twenty-first Century

What did I do wrong?

Addicts and alcoholics often zero in on Mom or Dad as the scapegoat—whether it's a teenager or an adult that has the problem. Rarely does a day go by that I don't get a call from a desperate parent, usually a mom, and find that the child has shifted some or all of their problems onto the parent. The insinuation from the addict to the parent is, *your parenting skills are the problem.* After a while, the parent may start to feel guilty and believe they are at least partly to blame. Ultimately the addict/alcoholic has found one more excuse to continue using—*it's my parent's fault.* The parent starts to think about what they could have done differently, and guilt builds. Often parents don't seek the help and support they need because of the shame they take upon themselves for not *preventing* this. So my advice is this: Don't start playing the *could've, would've, and should've game.* It can go on forever.

Parenting skills are important, and raising children is a big responsibility. Just the same, our kids make choices. *Taking the blame for another person's poor decisions solves nothing.* Some of their choices are good, and some not so good. Taking the blame for another person's poor decisions solves nothing. In fact when parents do this, they rob their child of the valuable lessons the consequences are meant to bring.

Mary, a friend of our family, has a son who, when he was seventeen, left home a few days before Christmas. The son had been abusing drugs and alcohol and when given the choice of living at home or using drugs, he chose to leave. Mary was doing her best to hold herself and the rest of her family together during the holidays. While attending a Christmas party, she confided in her neighbor, and the neighbor quickly remarked, "That kind of thing would never happen to us; we have much higher standards!"

A remark like this, which attempts to place the blame on the parents, can be incredibly damaging not only to the parents but to the child as well, shifting the blame in the wrong direction.

We should love our children, empathize with them, never give up hope, pray for them and do whatever we can to help them see the light. In spite of our best efforts, raising children in the twenty-first century in some ways can be like a roll of the dice. We've all seen cases where kids who came from horrible and abusive backgrounds have gone on to succeed in life. Unfortunately, the opposite also happens. There are no guarantees in child-rearing. Most of us do the best we can with information we have. Hindsight is 20/20, and often we learn as we go. If we, as parents, could go back in time and do some things differently, would we? Sure. Would that have eliminated all the problems our teens are having now? We'll never know, but I doubt it.

> *This is the culture you're raising your kids in.*
> *Don't be surprised if it blows up in your face.*
>
> —*Marilyn Manson*

Be Involved

My advice to parents is to stay involved in your children's daily lives, and be aware of some of the peer influences they are dealing with.

The social pressures are quite different from those you experienced as a teen, so make sure you take time to educate yourself—try to mentally enter their culture to gain a better understanding of it, and of them. Remember it is okay for you to know what is in your child's room and what they are doing while living under your roof. You can do your best to keep them safe and teach them to be wise. Also know that you cannot monitor their actions while they are away from home. Decisions that your teens make, good or bad, are what they learn from as they mature. Parents would love to be assured that their children will make all the best decisions, but as we all know, this will not always be the case.

When Judy and I were having problems with our son, Jake, we attended a seminar on parenting teens. I sat there for about two hours thinking, *I have heard this all before—many times, actually.* Finally, as the instructor was wrapping up, she said something that made me perk up. She said that in some cases, it's just a matter of getting them *from point A to point B,* meaning from adolescence to young adulthood.

> *Do what you feel in your heart to be right,*
> *for you'll be criticized anyway.*
> *You'll be damned if you do,*
> *and damned if you don't.*
>
> —*Eleanor Roosevelt*

There are powerful influences on our teenagers today that rival the authority of parents. Though you may feel that your efforts are futile, being an interested parent *is* important to your teenager, although their actions may appear to say quite the opposite. Approach the parent/child relationship with all the love, intelligence, and empathy that you can muster. However, regardless of your best efforts, keep in mind that ultimately you are not in control. Do not beat yourself up over your children's bad choices. Continue to be there for support, but most of all, don't let anyone make you believe that this is "all your fault."

I might add one more thing—don't expect perfection. Allow them to have some form of rebellion. By that I mean "pick your battles." Let them off the hook once in a while.

> *Fathers, do not aggravate your children, or they will become discouraged.*
>
> —*Colossians 3:21 (NLT)*
>
> *There's nothing wrong with a child that an arguing parent can't make worse.*
>
> —*Jim Fay, Love and Logic*

Chapter 14
What's Love Got to Do with It?

What works, what doesn't, and why.

Few things are more frustrating than watching someone's life spinning out of control because of substance abuse and addiction. If this same person had cancer, heart disease, or diabetes, they would be willing to do whatever was necessary to treat it. But the addict/alcoholic will both deny the existence of his problem and refuse treatment. This is one of the reasons why addiction is often referred to as cunning, baffling, and powerful.

> *All dope can do for you is kill you*
> *...the long hard way.*
> *And it can kill the people you love*
> *right along with you.*
> —Billie Holiday

Now as a concerned loved one, you probably want a clear answer to the question, *what do I do?*

How can a family member help?
1. Find help
2. Empathize
3. Talk to them about getting help

4. Expect resistance
5. Intervene
6. Pray

Find Help

First, get a friend, family member, pastor, youth group leader or professional involved who has dealt with the dynamics of addiction. The problem is too big to handle on your own. Gaining knowledge through books, seminars, "open"AA and Al-Anon meetings are great ways to learn more. Whatever resource you use, be sure the person you are listening to is trained or has personal experience with addiction. Psychiatrists, psychologists, and pastors may be helpful only if they have training or experience. In the recent past, none of these professions has required even one class on addiction.

> "If someone is faced with the problem of family members using drugs, I believe they need to give this person a lot of love.... Have patience and don't put them down all the time. Try to show them it isn't hopeless—that there are good places with good people that want to help them. Then assure them that you believe in their strength, and you know they can do it. God is important too. They need to ask Him for help daily."
>
> —*Gladys Herzanek*

The role of a family member or friend is an important one. Very few men or women seek help for addiction on their own, and most often family and close friends are the ones with the time and energy it takes to intervene. What works? The goal is to help someone to recognize the problem and seek help. How can you do that?

Empathize

No one plans on becoming drug-dependent. There is a stigma or sense of shame that is associated with such a lifestyle. Some in society still think of this as a mental health problem and that addicts are weak, bad, or crazy. So if you begin by trying to understand how this person is thinking and feeling and refrain from judging them, you've already taken a big step in the right direction.

Talk to Them About Getting Help

When talking to someone about this, the best approach is to plan in advance what you are going to say. Ask some questions, and then listen. Mention concerns you may have or changes you have observed. Plan when you will try to talk to him or her, at a time when you won't be interrupted. If you're dealing with an adolescent, make sure you aren't around their friends or peers. My wife and I have learned this the hard way, as we've discovered most teens have an image or persona that must not be challenged around friends. Doing so only invites conflict.

Expect Some Resistance

Even if the person is aware of the problem, they may still not want to quit. Quitting means a lot of change. The thought of living life substance-free is scary. When they feel pressure to quit, they might lie about their use, or try to convince you they can do it on their own. They may run away or isolate themselves from friends and family. They also may overcompensate by showing the world how *together* they are by working harder on the job or getting good grades in school. It may take many conversations spanning a period of weeks or months, so keep the lines of communication as open as you can.

There may be some occasions when you just take a break from trying to help. Much of this will depend on how severe the problem has become and how many other people are affected. Are children involved? Is a marriage failing? Are there legal or career concerns? Family members and friends need to encourage and support each other—there is strength in numbers.

Intervene

What do you do when you have spoken to this person and it still is not working? What's next? Some type of formal or informal intervention should be attempted. By this I mean using a professional interventionist. You might be surprised to find that they are able to pose options you haven't considered. Addiction and recovery is their area of expertise. They have heard every excuse from addicts and know how to respond most effectively. An interventionist can also be extremely persuasive and motivating. Call a treatment center and ask for this kind of help. Most will have a staff person that will do this at no cost.

The traditional intervention includes a training session for family members and other participants to equip them in ways to approach the addict. Often, the interventionist will meet the family and go over everything in advance—when to do it, what everyone should do to prepare, and what to say. Sometimes role-playing the entire event first is also effective.

The next step is the actual intervention. All the prep work has been done, the day and time chosen and the plans finalized for getting the addict to the meeting place—including an alternate day and place. Usually someone who knows their daily routine is selected to bring the user to the meeting. Most often, but not always, the addict docs not know the real reason he is being taken there. Once everyone is together, the interventionist will facilitate the meeting. Each person will speak, or read from a prepared statement, detailing why they love or care for this person, and how their abuse has affected his or her life. This can be a very emotional time; preparation is extremely important. Any potential objections that the addict may have concerning entering treatment will be anticipated. The interventionist's job is to guide the process. He will keep emotions in check and see that the outcome is successful.

A successful intervention is followed by a referral (and an escort, if necessary) to an appropriate treatment facility. The main focus is to get the person into treatment. Most of the time arrangements will have been made in advance so that taking time off work, childcare, and payment for treatment are not issues.

> *Bad times have a scientific value.*
> *These are occasions a good learner*
> *would not want to miss.*
>
> —*Ralph Waldo Emerson*

Remain Hopeful

Okay, so you have done *all the above* and nothing is working. What now? Do you quit trying? No. You may need to pull back for a while—maybe even for a long while; but remember, you need to remain hopeful that change will eventually happen. I know how difficult this can be. The few short years when we pulled back and waited for our son to take responsibility were very frustrating. It was not always easy to be optimistic. For our son, pain ended up being the best teacher. God was working "behind the scenes" in ways we never would have planned or even imagined.

Many men and women will fight with their alcohol/addiction problem until they are mentally and physically depleted. That is when the recovery process will begin.

What Doesn't Work?

When attempting to help our friend or loved one, we can often do the wrong thing. Because we are naturally motivated by love, and hate to see someone we care about suffer, we may be tempted to help too much. Often we will want to assist with an addict's physical and financial needs. A drug problem will often deplete a heavy user's resources. Loaning money, paying utility bills, fixing the car, calling their boss to say they are sick, are all counter-productive.

If this person hasn't stopped using, then all of this *helping* can really be *enabling*. Our good deeds are enabling our friend to continue using, and therefore delaying recovery. Don't rob your friend or loved one of the wonderful learning experience they are about to have. Part of normal human nature is to want to help someone in trouble, but we must begin to see this kind of "help" for what it is—harmful.

It's not easy to trust the process when we aren't seeing any improvement. Being patient can seem like work, and it is. Hang in there. Keep the faith. It's when things seem at their worst that we are inclined to give up. But in reality such struggles are moving the addict toward a better life.

Pray

Never underestimate the power of prayer.

God will light your path, one step at a time.

—Alan Ahlgrim, Lead Pastor
Rocky Mountain Christian Church, Niwot, CO

Part 2 Overview:
Key Points to Remember

- Do not try to fix someone's substance abuse problem by yourself.

- An intervention doesn't need to be complicated.

- Never give up hope.

- Pray.

- Know when to step back and allow consequences to happen.

- Do not allow siblings to be overlooked when an abuser is in the spotlight.

- Addiction is a physical, mental and spiritual brain disease.

- Addiction creates limited choice in people.

- Isolation becomes part of an abuser's life.

- Parents often wrongly feel that they are to blame for their children's substance abuse problems.

- Have empathy for the substance abuser, not sympathy.

- When trying to help, expect some resistance.

All About Treatment

Chapter 15
Different Strokes for Different Folks

Does treatment have to cost a lot?

Addiction crosses all education levels—from Yale to jail. IQ has little to do with it. Some of the lucky ones recognize the problem early, swallow their pride, and seek help. The majority, though, are like me. By that I mean they have an attitude—an attitude that says, "No one is going to tell me what to do!" One person may need only a few counseling sessions. Another might need a few months in a residential setting. Many centers offer outpatient and *intensive* outpatient treatment as well as residential treatment.

Inpatient or residential treatment is one option, though it is the most expensive. Even at discounted rates many families cannot afford a *28-day program*. However, this isn't necessary for every drug-dependent person. In fact, more than half of all recovering people didn't have the inpatient experience. As I make this point, please bear in mind that I'm not suggesting that inpatient treatment isn't beneficial. It would be wonderful if this was available to everyone; but it's not. There just aren't enough facilities for the demand. Even if there were, many people can't afford it.

Let's talk about a few other ways to begin recovery. Determining which treatment is appropriate will depend on the drugs the addict has been using, how much, for how long, and his or her level of motivation. We will start with the simplest and work our way up.

Counseling

For those who experience intervention early, before the addiction has become severe, the recovery process might be less complicated. It may involve only a couple of counseling sessions with an addiction counselor and then committing to attend recovery group meetings. There will be some who commit to recovery sooner than others, and the sooner, the better. Some people are lucky enough to not have to hit a "low bottom" (see chapter 18).

> ### No one is immune from addiction; it afflicts people of all ages, races, classes and professions.
> —*Patrick J. Kennedy*

Outpatient Treatment

For those with a moderate problem, outpatient treatment may be appropriate. This works well for the high-functioning addict/alcoholic. By high-functioning I mean the user still has a job and a home, pays his bills on time and is generally responsible, yet knows he has a real problem. Maybe a spouse or a friend has noticed his excessive drinking and mentioned something about it. If the dependent person is doing well on the job or in school and just can't leave for a month, outpatient treatment may be the answer. This candidate would attend group meetings, typically in the evenings and maybe also see a counselor a few times a week.

Intensive Outpatient Treatment

The next level of treatment is what is called *intensive* outpatient treatment. This usually consists of two-hour group meetings three to five nights a week. A professional addiction counselor facilitates the meeting. Again, the advantage here is that the addict can continue going to school or work and return to his or her home at night. This is a long day, but is an ideal solution for some who need daily support to be successful in recovery. It also is much less expensive, than residential treatment because the treatment center does not have to provide housing and meals. This option usually lasts four to six weeks and tapers down to whatever is best for the individual.

Inpatient/Residential Treatment

For serious cases, inpatient or residential treatment may be the best option. Residential treatment is what worked for me. I believe it is exceptionally effective for several reasons. First, it pulls the patient completely out of their environment, removing them from their friends, who are usually other substance abusers. A family may also want to consider sending the user out of state to *really* move them to a different environment (at this point, we are talking about only a few hundred extra dollars for traveling expenses).

Inpatient treatment is very structured. The first few days are often referred to as "detox,"which means going through some physical withdrawal. This phase varies quite a bit from person to person. Believe me, this experience is not fun, but I made it through. The severity of a person's detox experience depends on the drug or drugs a person has been using. I've heard a few people say it was no big deal at all. Others have described it as four or five days of *living hell*. There are some drugs available now that can help ease the discomfort of the first few days of withdrawal.

When I arrived at the treatment center in Atchison, Kansas, the intake person asked me about my drug use history. Along with everything else, I had been taking a high dose of Valium every day. I didn't think it was going to be a big deal to give up. But stopping this drug all at once, after years of use, was a shock to my system. I had a couple of *very* difficult days. The feelings I had are not easy to describe. Along with the insomnia came some hallucinations. In some ways it was like having a nightmare while being awake. The rational part of my brain knew I needed to quit using, not just Valium, but everything else as well. But my body and part of my mind still wanted and needed that drug. There was a battle going on. A real fight. Had I tried to do this on my own, I seriously doubt that I would have stuck it out.

Treatment centers want to move everyone through this stage as quickly as possible and get them involved in recovery work.

Most facilities post their regular schedule on their website. The lectures and groups that take place throughout the day shed light on every aspect of drug and alcohol dependency. The person learns in great detail what will happen (or has already happened) to them physically, mentally and spiritu-

> *Had I tried to do this on my own, I seriously doubt that I would have stuck it out.*

ally. In addition to participating in groups, each person meets one-on-one with a professional counselor. Many facilities have a chaplain on staff. Few, if any, chaplains will get into debating religion or suggest that a person must adopt any certain belief system. Regardless of this, people often come into treatment looking for answers to spiritual issues, and centers have found it beneficial to have a professional available to meet the spiritual needs of their patients.

I will always remember how meaningful it was to spend time during the evenings and weekends with others who shared the same struggles. There is a special bond among those who have *been there*. People are encouraged to take walks and to experience their feelings on a deeper level through journaling. Time allotted for reading, reflecting, prayer, and meditation are luxuries the addict did not have (and did not care about having) in his home environment. This experience can be a real turning point in a person's life.

> *Friendship is born at the moment*
> *one person says to another,*
> *"What! You too?*
> *I thought I was the only one!"*
>
> —C.S. Lewis

Specialized Treatment

Gender-specific (all-men or all-women) centers have recently become a great option. A patient who is in a gender-specific facility has the advantage of speaking more openly and gaining a more complete understanding from group members who share the same life experiences. There are certain issues that apply to men more than women, and vice versa. When addiction issues are dealt with in a specifically male or female context, a very therapeutic and powerful camaraderie forms.

Men, for example, find it difficult to admit weakness and accept defeat. But if they are with a group of other men who have also had their lives destroyed by drug abuse, they are more likely to be humble and honest in a group setting. Having to admit to brokenness in a mixed group is much more difficult—it's that whole *macho thing*. Even the reason men and women become users can be different. Men seem to take illicit drugs to get a high and as an adventure, whereas women take them more often to relieve stress and to self-medicate.

Women in treatment often have been taken advantage of by men, so they may be more likely to open up without men in the room. They are more sensitive to the social stigma of addiction, and therefore may have been more private about their substance use than men. Women also are more likely to be dealing with parenting issues. Lately, more and more inpatient treatment centers are opening their facilities to children so they can stay with their mothers for the duration of their treatment.

Depending on the severity of a person's addiction, longer treatment can be more effective than a typical twenty-eight-day stay. Sixty-day and ninety-day treatments are becoming more common. Someone who was using large amounts of methamphetamine, cocaine, or heroin over a period of years may need ninety days of treatment. But regardless of the drug the person has been using, there can be varying reasons why extended treatment may be to their advantage. For example,

There is a special bond among those who have "been there."

some people will need more time to work on ways to resist drug use and develop replacements for drug-using activities. There are many factors to consider before a person leaves treatment; the center itself will make recommendations. I can't think of any cases where a few extra weeks in treatment turned out to be a bad idea. There is a lot at stake here.

Cost of Treatment

In today's unstable economy, the financial strain of recovery is a real issue for families. How much does treatment have to cost? Who pays?

The average cost for a one-month program is about $20,000. Prices usually begin around $10,000 and go up to $40,000 or more. This is a lot of money—seemingly out of reach for most families. But when you consider how much money the addict has blown on drug and alcohol use in the past, and how beneficial this treatment program will be, it may be well worth it.

There are ways to defray the cost of treatment. First of all, some em- ployers are willing to help cover the cost; all you have to do is ask. Some insurance companies will cover the cost as well, so families need to find out what their insurance plan will and will not cover. However, many treatment facilities unfortunately do not accept insurance. Dealing with insurance companies is often a paperwork nightmare, and some centers do not have the staff to keep up with what it requires. Moreover, some insurance companies try to dictate just what type of treatment they will cover and for how long, and this may not fit with a treatment center's philosophy or diagnosis. However, there are centers that do take insurance, and usually they will make all the phone calls concerning coverage and handle the details for you.

If the employer won't help cover the cost of a treatment program, and the insurance plan doesn't cover it—or if it does but the treatment center won't accept insurance money—you should know that many facilities will take people for less than the standard fee—sometimes much less. Occasionally, patients are able to get ten to fifty percent off of the normal rate. Some centers will even let you make payments on a discounted price. In these cases, they are essentially loaning you the money in spite of credit history. How do you find out about these discounts? Ask. That's right, simply ask if there is any way to get a reduced fee.

How are they able to charge less? There may be some scholarship money available, or sometimes a hospital or a graduate of the treatment program will help cover the cost. If a treatment center sees that a person is able to pay only a portion of the cost, and if it is obvious that the person is motivated to begin recovery, those at the center will be motivated to help as

> *How do you find out about these discounts? Ask.*

well. For people working in this field, drug treatment is both a business and a passion. A high percentage of counselors, staff and owners are also recovering people. For most, it's not all about the money. Call around. Ask a lot of questions. You just might be surprised what you find out.

So far we've covered the more formal, structured treatment methods. So, what other forms of treatment or support are available?

> *In sobriety they teach you*
> *to think the drink through.*
> *Think through to the next morning,*
> *how it's going to influence you,*
> *the shame, how it's going to trigger*
> *the domino effect.*
>
> —*Charlie Sheen*

Twelve-Step Programs

Probably the most obvious are the twelve-step programs. AA (Alcoholics Anonymous) and NA (Narcotics Anonymous) are literally everywhere, all the time, across the world, and they are free. Al-Anon is also available to the family member who needs support or information. These groups all have listed phone numbers and will give you information twenty-four hours a day.

Sadly, within the Christian Community there are some who see a conflict with The Twelve Steps (of AA and Al-Anon) and biblical principles. I've studied this at length and I have found none. For those who are followers of Christ, we can simply know that He is our Higher Power—*our understanding of God.*

As I mentioned earlier, many churches are now adding addiction counselors to their staff. Some churches even refer to themselves as "Recovery Churches." Things are changing. An important point to keep in mind is that the addict or alcoholic must have *daily* support as they begin this road to recovery. In the beginning, a person in recovery is high-maintenance and needs daily support. This is why I believe that a twelve-step program *must* be part of early recovery. Are there rare exceptions to this? Yes. But remember how much is at stake. I personally know of many Christians who took advantage of what AA had to offer and are now glad they did.

Is AA or NA appropriate for everyone? This is a tough question. You can surely check it out for yourself. Discourage your friend or family member from making a judgment too quickly after visiting just one group. Each group has its own personality. Sometimes it takes visiting several to find a group that the addict will feel comfortable with. There are different meetings in all parts of town, including: men's, women's, open meetings (where a person doesn't have to be an alcoholic to attend), and speaker meetings.

Some people in certain professional fields might not feel comfortable attending AA or NA meetings, even though the names of those attending, and the content of such meetings, are confidential. Why? Some people are very visible in their community. If a person is a doctor, dentist, police officer, city official, pastor, judge, lawyer, school-teacher, swim coach, school counselor, CEO, pharmacist, pilot, or bus driver, it might be very difficult to stay anonymous. Most people wouldn't want to jeopardize their career to get support in such a potentially public manner. I wouldn't want to meet my surgeon at an AA meeting! Some people may need to find a different resource, but more often than not, twelve-step groups are very beneficial.

Spin-offs of the traditional twelve-step groups include faith-based groups like *Celebrate Recovery, Christians in Recovery* and the Salvation Army. The Salvation Army also offers free in-patient recovery programs in some cities.

There is help available for almost everyone. People that need recovery have choices, ranging from those that cost absolutely nothing to a multitude of deluxe high-priced options. Help is out there. Just ask.

Over the past two decades I've seen addicts and families recover from both mild and severe addiction problems. Sadly, there are others who give up the fight before they even get started. Finding a good support group or counselor doesn't always happen overnight. Get referrals, talk to others who had similar problems, and be persistent. Determination always pays off.

There is help available for almost everyone. People that need recovery have choices.

Chapter 16
One Step at a Time?

Are twelve-step meetings really important?

> *Two are better than one . . .*
> *If one falls down,*
> *his friend can help him up.*
> *But pity the man who falls*
> *and has no one to help him up!*
>
> —*Ecclesiastes 4:9-10*

Does a person have to attend twelve-step meetings to recover? Are they necessary to maintain long-term recovery? There is no short answer to this question but it is a lot harder to recover without them. I have attended many twelve-step meetings all across the country. These meetings come in different sizes, ranging from a few people to a few hundred. Some groups seem to develop their own personalities. Meetings are sometimes designed around various groupings and categories, such as smoking and non-smoking. Others are broken down into age categories, and some are gender-specific. Twelve-step meetings have been in existence since 1935, with more meetings being added all the time. It may take someone a while to find a group that they feel comfortable attending. This is the same as looking for a health club, book club, or church. No one particular group is going to be perfect. It is senseless to search forever. Finding a group that is just "okay" is a good start.

You may need to remind your loved one that everyone attends twelve-step meetings

No one particular group is going to be perfect.

for the same reason. Those committed to a group are there to help themselves and also to help others stay drug and alcohol-free. Everyone who goes to these meetings does so voluntarily, but it is common to feel awkward in the beginning. As I mentioned earlier, try a few different meetings, and then decide which to attend regularly.

In the beginning, right after leaving treatment, I wasn't very excited about going to any kind of support group. I felt awkward and out of place. When I did go, I rarely spoke at all, and took a back seat. Eventually, after several weeks, I did get to the place where I enjoyed being part of the group. I began to participate in discussions, and even looked forward to the meetings.

You may find that the recovering person in your life chooses to avoid attending a group altogether. Unfortunately, this is not the best choice, because it often leaves them all alone in the recovery process, with no one to hold them accountable. Twelve-step meetings offer consistent encouragement, empathy, advice, and role models that other alternatives do not provide. The familiar saying is true: An addict all by himself is in bad company.

> *We will lose interest in selfish things*
> *and gain interest in our fellows.*
>
> —*Alcoholics Anonymous*

Those beginning recovery need other recovering people to talk to for support. There is no substitute for one person helping another. Hurting people need to know that the person trying to help them has been there and that they speak from experience. This applies more so with addiction than with most other challenges. I can't think of any other problem anyone can face that is so sensitive in this way. Most men and women new to recovery would rather talk to a high-school dropout with six months of sobriety than to a PhD who has authored ten books on the subject but who has never had an addiction problem.

I'm not saying that a trained counselor or pastor is unable to help a person in recovery. There are many wonderful counselors in the addiction field who are not in recovery and who can offer valuable insights. In fact, they are able to let us know when we may not be getting the best advice from a fellow recovering person. Usually a combination of both—clinical expertise and support from another recovering person—is the best choice.

Back to our original question: *Are twelve-step meetings essential?*

Here are the steps we took,
which are suggested as a program of recovery

1) We admitted we were powerless over alcohol, that our lives had become unmanageable.

2) Came to believe that a Power greater than ourselves could restore us to sanity.

3) Made a decision to turn our will and our lives over to the care of God as we understood Him.

4) Made a searching and fearless moral inventory of ourselves.

5) Admitted to God, to ourselves, and to another human being the exact nature of our wrongs.

6) Were entirely ready to have God remove all these defects of character.

7) Humbly asked Him to remove our shortcomings.

8) Made a list of all persons we had harmed, and became willing to make amends to them all.

9) Made direct amends to such people wherever possible, except when to do so would injure them or others.

10) Continued to take personal inventory and when we were wrong promptly admitted it.

11) Sought through prayer and meditation to improve our conscious contact with God as we understood Him, praying only for knowledge of His will for us and the power to carry that out.

12) Having had a spiritual awakening as the result of these steps, we tried to carry this message to alcoholics, and to practice these principles in all our affairs.

—AA Twelve Steps

My belief is that everyone in recovery can and will benefit from being part of some therapeutic community—especially in the beginning. Does it have to be AA or NA? Not all the time. For some it can be groups such as those offered in outpatient care, facilitated by a trained addiction counselor. These are structured groups as well. But no matter what method of recovery an addict chooses, it is crucial to understand the significance of support. Remember that we are talking about a disease that can be fatal—a disease that will try to convince someone he is *cured* and no longer needs help when in fact he does.

> ### *Friendship ... is not something you learn in school.*
> ### *But if you haven't learned the meaning of friendship,*
> ### *you really haven't learned anything.*
> —*Muhammad Ali*

Another effective option may be to choose a recovery group through a local church, if one is available. These groups are becoming more and more common, and provide support for the addict as well as offering groups for family members.

Others in recovery may opt for one-on-one sessions with a counselor. These options still provide needed support. What is important to keep in mind is the *insidiousness* of addiction. Addiction may try to convince a person that they can handle their problem on their own. I have yet to meet someone who has truly been able to recover alone. There are people who have *quit or stopped using* all by themselves, but what I don't see in these people is the serenity or peace of mind that comes with *real* recovery. My belief is that being part of a group of like-minded people for a period of time is critical for true success. No group has been more successful than the 12-step AA model.

Which support group is best, and how often and for how long someone may need to attend, will vary. I have two very good friends who went
to the same treatment center that I went through. Both of them attended
a few meetings of support groups after they finished their twenty-eight
day programs. For them, that approach worked and they have been drug-
free ever since. My story is much different. I regularly attended support
groups—along with church for more than a few years. Outpatient meetings
offered by Valley Hope and twelve-step groups were the two resources
that worked well for me. What works for one person may not be right for
another. Each recovering person must decide for himself or herself what
method is most effective. Regardless of what we may need to do to stay
sober, it is usually a small price to pay when compared to the destruction of
active addiction. A few hours a week spent on recovery, even if we have
to continue this until the day we die, is not a big deal.

My suggestion is to keep an open mind about attending support
groups. After a while, the recovering addict usually starts to *enjoy* going.
I know this may sound crazy, but it is true.

My wife, Judy, also has more than twenty-five years of success in recovery. We enjoy going to meetings together. Our kids like to joke about
how when we are on vacation in a new city or town, we will often find
a meeting to attend: "All our friends' parents go out dancing or to a bar
when they are on vacation, and what do our parents do for fun? They go
to AA meetings!" It's true. A recovering person can walk into an AA (or
NA) meeting anywhere *in the world* and instantly be accepted by a room
full of strangers. After the hour is over, he finds that he now has a whole
room full of friends!

As a result of going to meetings, an addict's attitude begins to change:
he develops friendships, sees growth in himself, and notices the growth
of the participants around him. The skeptic who once was afraid to walk
through the doors begins to enjoy recovery and enjoy life.

Chapter 17

Step One:
Don't Leave Home Without It!

What's the big deal about Step One?

> *We admitted that we were powerless over alcohol*
> *and that our lives had become unmanageable.*
> —*Step One, AA 12-Steps*

Whether you are a fan of twelve-step programs or not, the first step an attendee will hear offers a great deal of wisdom. The alcoholic/addict should never venture into the world without remembering the important bit of knowledge that *Step One* provides: Chemically dependent people will never be able to gain control over their substance use. Millions of addicted people have tried, and many have even died trying. **Not one truly addicted person** has ever successfully returned to social use.

Admitting Powerlessness

After many years in recovery, I know that I *must* not forget this one principle—I will always be an addict. Confusion on this matter can lead to disastrous results. My substance use took me places I didn't want to go, cost me more than I wanted to pay and kept me longer than I wanted to stay. My addiction is now in remission. Just the same, it is alive and well—ready to inflict a lot of pain on me. To forget this would be my greatest mistake.

I have a friend who owns a treatment center in the Colorado Rocky Mountains called Jaywalker Lodge. He accepts only men who are highly motivated to change. The program is a three-month-minimum-stay facility in which the primary focus is to fully

> *After many years in recovery, I know that I must not forget this one principle—I will always be an addict.*

personalize Step One, in order to move forward with the following steps. It's for men who have made several attempts to quit, only to find themselves stumbling again and again. Frustrated and broken, they arrive at the treatment center willing to do whatever it takes to regain their sobriety. This facility teaches men that the key to recovery starts with a true admission of powerlessness.

Once a recovering addict is convinced of their inability to ever control their using, they will no longer attempt to do so if they want to maintain their recovery. Incorporating Step One into a person's life requires a daily ongoing shift in thinking—sometimes referred to as "one day at a time." Lifelong recovery obviously involves much more than this one crucial admission. Recovery and rebuilding what was lost takes substantial time and effort. But it will all be in vain if this one fundamental principle is forgotten.

> *God grant me the serenity*
> *to accept the things*
> *I cannot change;*
> *Courage to change the things I can;*
> *and wisdom to know the difference.*
>
> *—Reinhold Niebuhr*

A Humbling Realization

Once the power or ability to control how much a person can use is lost, it is lost forever. Any attempt to regain control is futile. This applies to the user who is brand new to recovery as well as to someone with over two decades of abstinence. No one is tougher than addiction. You, as a person close to the situation, should understand this fundamental step as a foundational principle. It's a humbling realization.

> *When one door closes, another door opens;*
> *but we often look so long and so regretfully*
> *upon the closed door, that we do not see*
> *the ones which open for us.*
>
> —*Alexander Graham Bell*

Chapter 18
Pivotal Teaching Moments

The "rock bottom" myth.

> *Drugs are a waste of time.*
> *They destroy your memory*
> *and your self-respect*
> *and everything that goes along with*
> *your self-esteem.*
> —Kurt Cobain

Yeah, when he hits bottom he'll be ready.
A user has to hit bottom before he will change.
Sooner or later she will hit bottom. Then she'll be ready to get some help.

Raise the Bottom

This whole idea of "hitting bottom" is out of date. Some people will wait years—even decades—for their friend to reach this mythical point in their alcohol and drug use. But why wait for them to "hit bottom"? Why not help them by *raising* their bottom? There are ways to encourage someone to reach for help much earlier. In doing so, we can avoid a lot of unnecessary pain and heartache—and maybe even save their life. For some people, hitting bottom will be six feet underground.

I'll use my son as an example. Jake is a great kid, grew up in a Christian home, attended church camps and is doing well in college. He's studying and has found a major that he is excited about. He also works at a part-time job where he has recently been promoted to manager. We are extremely proud of him.

But life hasn't always been this promising for Jake. He began his early teen years pretty much as I did. At age thirteen, Jake began to experiment with alcohol and pot. He did this in spite of the fact that his father was an addiction counselor (or maybe subconsciously *because* of it, since that would be a good way to rebel against Dad). Jake was also very aware of how genetic predisposition could play a role in his life, as he knew my own addiction story well. However, he made some wrong choices, which to me reconfirmed that there was some truth to the genetic correlation.

At times he was out of control, and as a result he was often suspended from school. He got in trouble for fighting and pulling the fire alarm during school. He even managed to get a ticket for reckless driving in the school parking lot. He and some friends tore up a golf course one night with a 4 x 4 truck. He was also selling drugs. One night we had four police cars in front of our house when he was arrested, and they searched our house with a drug-sniffing dog. His probation officer came by frequently, and he had to take random UAs (urine analysis tests for drugs). At one point, he couldn't leave the house for several weeks because he had an ankle bracelet (a monitoring device on his leg as part of one of his probation requirements), so he figured he would sell drugs out of our house.

Eventually the principal of his high school told him, "We've had it, don't come back." Right before our eyes, he had almost turned into a stranger. Jake was frequently running away from home and running from police. He soon found his life swarming with issues he could not handle because of his substance use. For a time, Judy and I were on edge, just dreading to hear the phone ring. Someone was always calling us about Jake. Although his police problems were not major, we did often have a patrol car in our driveway. It was great excitement for the neighbors! We had many sleepless nights worried about our son's safety. At least four of his friends had been killed in alcohol-related incidents. *How long was this going to last? How much more trouble could he possibly get into?* This painful phase of drug abuse in my own life had gone on for sixteen years, which made me determined to help Jake all the more. I couldn't bear to see him go through the same thing I did. Judy and I pursued counseling, parenting seminars, and other resources for support.

Most of our attempts did little to help. There were some very low times for us. During one counseling session Jake got up and stormed out of the room. Nothing seemed to be the answer for our son. Though we continued to try, we learned that this was not something we could *control.* All we could do was hold things together and continue to hope and pray for Jake.

Addicts like me, and potentially my son, often need to learn things the hard way. Judy vividly recalls a time when Jake was about three years old. She was ironing and told him not to touch the iron—that it was hot. He looked directly into her eyes, stuck out his finger and touched it. At that moment she knew this was not going to be an easy road. Jake was going to have to learn things the hard way.

> ## *We cannot learn without pain.*
> *—Aristotle*

The Value of Pain

Pain can be a wonderful teacher. Pain usually means that something is wrong or perhaps broken. Without pain, most people would have even larger problems. Pain is a signal that we need to do something different if we want it to stop.

We decided to not rob Jake of these pivotal learning opportunities. We weren't going to lie for him, put up his bail, or pay for lawyers. In one of the seminars we attended, we were advised not to argue with our son; just let the consequences be the "bad guy." When the police brought him home late one night, we let the law take its course. A traffic infraction while Jake was on probation had turned into a search, and drugs were found in the car. The officers told me what happened and asked me what I wanted to do. Jake was a minor, under the age of eighteen, so I was still responsible for him. I asked them what they would normally do if we had not been home. The officer told me that the normal course of action would be to put him in jail. I said, "Okay, go ahead, and do what you would normally do if we were not here." I was told to pick him up in the morning.

> *Pain is temporary. It may last a minute, or an hour, or a day, or a year, but eventually it will subside and something else will take its place.*
>
> —*Lance Armstrong*

As parents, it wasn't easy to watch them put handcuffs on him and drive away. This would be the first of three incidents like this. Jake learned that we were not going to rescue him.

From then on, we allowed the natural consequences be his teacher. For ten days in January, he was sentenced to wilderness work camp (unofficially called *hoods in the woods*), where he slept in a tent high in the Rocky Mountains. He later spent ten days in juvenile detention, and we didn't bail him out or hire a lawyer. All this was painful for him and for us as well.

Jake didn't like being locked up, and he was beginning to connect the dots. But still, we endured a few more difficult years. Jake didn't change overnight and his problem continued to be a strain on our family. His problem was all-consuming, taking up the majority of our physical and mental energy for a time.

Eventually, Jake's substance use took its toll on our marriage, as we didn't always agree about what to do next. Judy was always willing to give Jake the benefit of the doubt. In an effort not to unjustly accuse Jake, she felt a need to almost be an eyewitness before she would accept his drug problem. Mountains of circumstantial evidence were not enough. I, on the other hand, looked at the situation differently. Although I wasn't an eyewitness, I was convinced that Jake had a substance abuse problem. This strained our relationship. Sometimes we were cold and silent, not communicating for days.

How did we make it through this? We remained committed to each other and to our marriage. We attended counseling, seminars, read books, prayed a lot and just plain "stuck it out," believing *this too shall pass.* Eventually it did.

It's not easy for a parent (especially a mom) to watch her child suffer—even when she knows it is exactly what is best for him. We believe the decisions we made concerning how to handle Jake's problems made a significant difference in his life. God was at work—behind the scenes.

> *Don't rob your friend or loved one of the wonderful learning experience they are about to have.*

Jake eventually graduated from a special high school, located in the Boulder court house outside of the juvenile court room. This school, Justice High, consists of kids whom many people have given up on. Their combination of encouragement and tough, structured guidance provides troubled youth with another chance. Jake played on the football team, graduated as class valedictorian and was inducted into the National Honor Society!

What could have gone on for many years was cut short. Sometimes our natural inclination is to rescue those we love, but often this is the most harmful thing we can do. For Jake, his big battle was from about age thirteen to seventeen. It could just as easily have been from ages thirteen to twenty-nine—just like his Dad. What did we do? *We raised his bottom.* We allowed the consequences to pile up fast. And we allowed Jake to take care of them himself. His personal victory over his struggles gives him great motivation and confidence as he now realizes that he has what it takes to succeed in life.

> "My parents tried to control me for years. I remember waking up to the sound of my dad sawing through my door at 7 o'clock in the morning, taking a big fat permanent marker and writing a date on my wall of which I had to get a job. My parents, mainly my father, tried to control me so much . . . and were so afraid that I would end up addicted like they were, that one time I had a rule sheet five pages long telling me when I was supposed to be home and what I could and couldn't do.
>
> . . . My life started to go downhill and out of control very quickly. I had never successfully gotten off probation . . . I had my parents worried, the police or someone's parents were always calling . . . From the time I got arrested for selling coke, I realized that this was basically my last straw with the court system. I finally decided to do what I had to do, to get off probation and stay out of jail. I got away with everything that I could, but I was smart enough to realize I was out of chances . . . I couldn't make any more mistakes."
>
> —*Jake Herzanek*

So does everyone have to hit rock bottom? I would say *no*. Tough love can prevent a substance abuser from prolonging their usage. There are loving ways to refuse to rescue someone that in the long run will help them to choose recovery. Loving means doing the right thing to help. This can take all of our strength and energy at times. We all hate to see someone suffer—even when the suffering is a consequence of their bad choices.

This approach, or some form of it, is something you might consider: Raise the bottom. Whether it is a teenage son or daughter, a spouse, boyfriend, aunt or uncle, the same principles can apply. A few nights in jail could be the best thing that ever happens to them.

The next time this person you care about appeals to you to get them out of a bind (loan them money, pay their electric bill, buy them gas, pay for a lawyer), think twice. You just might be prolonging their disease and robbing them of the natural consequences that they need to experience in order to seek help and begin to *connect the dots*.

> *Don't bail them out. A few nights in jail could be the best thing that ever happens to them.*

Chapter 19

Meth Myths

Can meth addicts really recover?

Methamphetamine is much different from regular amphetamine pills. Without going into a chemistry lesson, meth is simply a more refined or condensed form of amphetamine. It is much more powerful than what most people might think of as diet pills or speed. It produces both an intense feeling of energy and strong euphoric pleasure at the same time. Some of the intensity depends on how quickly it gets into the system. This drug in pill form, taken orally, is slow to produce this effect. Injecting or smoking it is a completely different experience. By smoking meth, large amounts of the drug can be dumped into the bloodstream, which is carried to the brain in a matter of seconds.

History

Developed in the late 1800s in Germany, the chemical make-up of methamphetamine has changed a few times over the years. Meth is an amphetamine drug that is prescribed for use in nasal decongestants and bronchial inhalers, treating narcolepsy, attention deficit disorder, and obesity. Prescribed under the name Desoxyn, this drug suppresses the appetite and increases energy levels, causing increased activity. For some people suffering from ADD, it has the opposite effect—slowing them down. Both legal and illegal use has been with us for many years.

Amphetamines (speed) was common back when I was using. Meth was more difficult to be found. During those years, cocaine was the drug of choice. When I used meth in pill form, I could definitely tell that it was not a typical form of speed. The effect was also much longer lasting.

Chasing the High

Before anyone runs out to try this, let me tell you more about it. With this drug, use turns to abuse, which turns to addiction *very quickly.* It's almost impossible to re-create that initial feeling of intense pleasure. We often hear the term *chasing the high,* meaning that once the user has this almost unbelievable experience, they want to repeat it. This is like trying to catch something that is always out in front of you, but never within reach. Chasing, running faster, and trying harder doesn't work— yet the user doesn't stop trying. *Chasing* that first euphoric experience can continue for a long time. In fact, some may die trying to catch it.

> *Some became fools through their rebellious ways*
> *and suffered affliction . . .*
> *They loathed all food and drew near*
> *the gates of death.*
>
> —*Psalm 107:17-18*

Consequences

This particular drug also has some devastating effects—both on the body and mind. It is not uncommon for users to stay awake and active for days at a time. After being up for several days, users will start to hallucinate, seeing what is referred to as "shadow people"—a type of hallucination that seems to be unique to users of this drug. People high on meth will often become paranoid and obsessive, thinking the police are watching them. One user told me he became so obsessed with the color black that he painted the entire interior of his house that color.

Another woman told me she thought her car radio was talking to her personally, and if a helicopter flew overhead she believed the people in it were watching her. Another man, who visited online chat rooms to arrange meetings for anonymous sex, said that the Internet is loaded with meth addicts looking for the same thing. This drug is straight out of Hell.

The physical consequences of meth use are more obvious: it eats away the enamel of the teeth and produces skin lesions. Lack of sleep and food for long periods of time will take its toll on the body and bring it to the point where it just can't function any longer. The drug will eventually stop working and the user may crash and sleep for days.

Does this sound like fun or what? I mean, why would you want all this to stop?

Recovery from Meth Addiction

Do people really recover from meth addiction? Can they recover?

You may have heard the myth, *People cannot recover from addiction to meth.* Why has the myth evolved? It is probably because meth use has exploded over the past decade. Meth labs and meth-driven crimes receive a lot of press coverage, so there is a general assumption that addiction to methamphetamine is out of control and there is no hope of recovery. People become addicted to meth more quickly than to various other drugs, and because of this, many are led to believe that nobody can get off this stuff. However, just because we have more and more people addicted to meth does not mean that they can't recover. People recover from this drug very frequently. In fact, the recovery rates for meth addiction are about the same as for other drugs such as cocaine, alcohol, and heroin.

Is meth use a big problem? Yes! Do people do some crazy things when they are high on this drug? Yes. Is this impacting the crime rate? Yes. Do people become violent and unpredictable on this drug? Yes.

But another yes is that people can and do recover from addiction to meth. It may require a longer period of treatment for recovery, and some of the physical damage from the drug may take longer to heal, but nonetheless, with hard work, determination and prayer people frequently get off this drug.

Recovery rates from addiction are about the same, regardless of the drug of choice. Heroin, alcohol, tobacco, painkillers, and meth all have one thing in common: If the *want to* is there, users can recover. This may sound simplistic or trite, but it is true. In fact, a former meth addict who is in long-term recovery once told me, "No one's case is special or unique. Those who *want to* quit badly enough can recover."

> *If the "want to" is there, people do recover. Sometimes they need to be coerced to seek help, and the "want to" comes much later, after a period of time.*

But what if a person doesn't *want to?* They may say they don't, because they can't imagine what life would be like without the drug, and they don't believe they could live without it. Sometimes they need to be coerced to seek help, and the *want to* comes much later, after a period of time in treatment. Treatment works for these people as well. Don't let anyone tell you it doesn't.

Michelle's story: Starting Over

Michelle grew up in a small town outside of Austin, Texas in a middle-class neighborhood with two older brothers and a younger sister. Tall and slender, with naturally wavy dark hair, Michelle was a popular girl who sang in choir and received average grades in school. There was not much to do in town, and most of the kids in high school went out drinking on the weekends. This small-town culture taught her quickly that if she wanted to have friends, she needed to hang out with kids who liked to party. At first she didn't even like the taste of alcohol, but eventually she learned to like it.

Meth had started to become popular and Michelle knew a few kids who were experimenting with it. Her new boyfriend had begun making it in an abandoned barn on his parents' farm, about a half-mile or so from his house. The fumes were bad at times, but the smell of livestock, and the distance of the barn from the house, made it so that no one noticed anything unusual.

At first, Michelle's boyfriend thought it was fun and exciting to try to make meth, kind of like a chemistry experiment. Of course, making extra money was another incentive. She said that he got to the point where he really liked the stuff as well. Before long, he was injecting it. "I never thought I would do that," Michelle confessed. "It seemed weird. He was always trying to get me to try it with him. Up until then, all I'd done was smoke pot and drink."

"One day, I still don't know why, but I said okay. I was scared, but excited at the same time. Right away the feeling was beyond anything I could imagine. For the next few months, getting high was all I could think about. Summer vacation had just started, so we were using it all the time. I was seventeen, and everything was changing fast. I was hooked, and meth was in control of me. I didn't go back to school in the fall. By then, my whole life had changed. My parents figured out what was going on. I left home, and my boyfriend and I moved into a crummy apartment with some people we hardly knew in Dallas—who were also users.

"The next six years were hell. My boyfriend was arrested and sent to prison. That left me with just a few friends, and we were all using meth. I didn't work, and just lived off other people. I didn't care what I looked like and I had lost so much weight that my arms were like sticks and my ribs were showing. My skin was pasty white, and sores developed on my body. My teeth had begun to rot away from using. I didn't want anyone in my family to see me, so I never went back home. What was happening to me was scary, but I didn't know any other way to live. Sometimes, I would call my mom when I was depressed. She knew what was going on and said that I should get some help—go to rehab. I hated the sound of that word, even though I knew my life was a mess.

"Finally, one evening there was a knock on our door. As it turned out, my brother had found out from some other people where I lived and came to see me. He took one look and insisted that I come home with him. To make a long story short, he made some phone calls and with the help of my family, I entered a treatment center run by the Salvation Army. By then I was willing to do whatever—as long as they promised me things would get better.

"That was three and a half years ago. I like myself again. It was so tough in the beginning. I knew a few people who had tried quitting, but kept going back to using. Treatment worked for me. I started feeling better slowly, and realized that my life didn't have to be the way it was. I began to care about how I looked again, started eating right and learned to ride a road bike—my newfound pastime. After the first year of my recovery, a local dentist offered to repair my teeth for a discounted rate. My smile is back!

"The most difficult thing, I think, for most people to understand is how this drug will mess up a person's thoughts. When someone begins to rely on a drug to make them feel good (or even just normal), and then when all of a sudden they don't have the drug, they have to learn to do everything sober—without anything to mask life's challenges. Things that make most people happy don't always affect me the same. Most people don't understand. That is why having friends in recovery is so important to me.

"In meetings, I meet a lot of people who were just like me, or even in worse shape. Every once in a while I hear someone say they went back and tried it again. Some people have just disappeared from coming to meetings and don't come back. It's sad. I don't know what happened to them. This is one of the great things about a support group. I can learn from the mistakes of others. There was one girl who I knew real well who died. We didn't see her for a few days, and then someone read about it in the paper. It was all over the news. We went to her funeral. She was only twenty-seven.

"I still have some down days, but nothing like before. I just make myself do what I need to do. My spiritual life is a big part of my recovery. I pray a lot, read lots of books and talk to my sponsor. Helping new people seems to help me also. Sometimes I think crazy thoughts about the past, and my relationships that formed around meth. My boyfriend was released from prison, but got in trouble again with meth. I have a new boyfriend now—we're both in recovery. My family has forgiven me as well, and I see my mom again. I don't know where my future will take me, but I feel like I have one. For those six years of my life, using meth, I just went from day to day with only one thing on my mind—using. I'm gonna make it. Now my one-day-at-a-time thoughts are much different."

> ... *"Everything is possible for him who believes."*
> —*Mark 9:23*

Chapter 20
Payback Time

What is withdrawal like?

> ### *Tell me it's cold outside and not just me.*
> ### *I'm uncomfortable.*
>
> —Pete Droge, *Spacey and Shakin'*

People are curious. People are afraid. *What is withdrawal like? What must someone be willing to do in order to recover?* Undoing the damage is going to take time. There is a price, and the down payment on a life in recovery is the decision to stop using drugs.

There is no instant cure. Let me repeat this for those who may have skimmed over it. *There is no instant cure.* This means that the substance user is going to experience withdrawal. Although most of the physical distress of this phase is over in a few days or less (sometimes more, depending on the various factors), it can seem like an eternity.

So what's it really like? Long periods of continued substance use directly affect the central nervous system (which consists of the brain and the spinal cord). Physical dependency happens when this part of our body has been altered. Drug withdrawal is both physical, psychological and spiritual.

The Physical Part of Withdrawal

The physical part of withdrawal is often accompanied by side effects. A person in recovery may experience any of the following: shaking hands, high blood pressure, irregular heart palpitations, panic attacks, hallucinations, and even seizures. This is the body's way of saying, *I'm not happy.* This is all part of the detox process. Over time, a person's body will build up a huge tolerance to drugs like alcohol, pain pills, tranquilizers, and others. It can get to the point where even a few hours of not using a drug will start to bring on withdrawal symptoms. Often when we hear someone say, "I need a drink," it is true. Their body *needs* another dose of whatever it is used to or withdrawal symptoms will begin. I know a woman in recovery who often had to leave a cart full of groceries in the store because she realized she couldn't sign her check without shaking.

One reason alcoholics drink throughout the day is because withdrawal symptoms come on rapidly.

Symptoms of Withdrawal

As I mentioned before, the severity of addiction and the type of drugs used will determine how difficult the withdrawal period will be. Everyone who goes through withdrawal finds that they experience reactions that are the exact opposite of what the drug normally did for them.

Withdrawal from Sedatives

For example, if a person used sedative/hypnotic drugs such as alcohol, heroin or pain pills, during withdrawal they would experience agitation, anxiety, and even pain. Physical symptoms could include higher blood pressure, sweating, and a racing heart. Alcohol and heroin withdrawal, though difficult, usually lasts for a shorter period of time, sometimes only a few days. Withdrawal from pain medications, such as Vicodin, Percocet and OxyContin, can take longer. People who have developed a high tolerance for drugs like OxyContin typically have a tougher time in withdrawal. But just the same, *people do get through it.*

> ### *I get spacey and shakin'*
> ### *Feel like I'm being taken away.*
> —Pete Droge, *Spacey and Shakin'*

There is another class of sedative-type drugs that can be equally diffi-cult to withdraw from: benzodiazepines, which are tranquilizers typically prescribed for anxiety or sleep disorders. The most well known in this group is probably Valium, but you may also have heard of Xanax, Libri-um, and Ativan. For someone who has experienced a traumatic event (e.g. divorce, or the death of someone close to them), these drugs can provide short-term help. However, if used for a long time they are very addicting, both physically and mentally. *I know what I'm talking about here.*

Over the years I used several different drugs. Valium was one I used consistently. When I couldn't find it from dealers, I called doctors. There were times when I would get out the phonebook, go down the list in the yellow pages and make several appointments. I would make up different stories, from "I'm going through a divorce" to "I can't sleep"—anything that I thought would work. In a few days, I would end up with six to ten prescriptions. I did not want to run out of this drug!

With alcohol, pain medications, and tranquilizers such as Valium, withdrawal symptoms can include anxiety, physical discomfort, seizures and sometimes panic attacks. Other side effects may include shaking, cold sweats, and even hallucinations. All of these diminish over time and then go away completely. During this process, there is very little a family member or friend can do to help. Most people in withdrawal would prefer to not have family or friends around to see them go through this.

Withdrawal from Stimulants
The opposite of the normal effects of stimulants (drugs like speed,

meth, and cocaine) would be depression, sadness, and a lack of energy. During withdrawal from stimulants, some people may sleep a lot, not want to get out of bed, and not enjoy activities that used to bring them pleasure. Most abusers of stimulants have an initial short period of *physical withdrawal.* This is to be expected. On a smaller scale, even people who quit drinking caffeinated coffee will complain of headaches during the first few days.

The psychological symptoms of withdrawal from stimulants last much longer—but are much less intense. The *mind game* phase goes on for some time. The depression from quitting meth or cocaine can be frustrating. The addict may feel as though his life

> *The "mind game" phase goes on for some time.*

will never be enjoyable again. His mind still seeks the intense high that it once experienced. This is one of the reasons why support groups are critical. Knowing that others are experiencing the same thoughts and feelings is reassuring, and sharing with others brings healing.

Withdrawal from Hallucinogens

Although marijuana is considered *mild* for this group and not very physically addicting, people do become dependent on it. However, there is very little, if any, physical withdrawal. Quitting marijuana use will often bring on some agitation, as well as some depression, leaving people feeling that the only way to have fun is to get high. These symptoms are not usually as severe as those of withdrawal from stronger drugs. Unfortunately, the long-term damage caused from this particular drug poses other problems for the user, such as loss of memory, difficulty learning new skills and lack of motivation.

LSD, Ecstasy, and mushrooms are much stronger, but the good news is that it is rare to see anyone addicted to these drugs. LSD produces such intense hallucinations that most people will use it only occasionally and typically stop once they've experienced a "bad trip," which can be a terrorizing experience. During the sixteen years that I've worked in jails and prisons, only one man said that his drug of choice was LSD. He was kept in the area of the jail designated "Special Management."

For any drug, physical consequences of withdrawal should be expected and even planned for. When I went through it, I was miserable for several days. For people who use several different drugs, withdrawal may include all the symptoms I have mentioned. Just the same, people do survive the experience and *do recover.*

Once an addict has gone through the physical and mental anguish of detox, negative memories that remain with him may help serve as motivation to not use, as this painful time isn't something he wants to endure again. In today's treatment centers, the detox and withdrawal symptoms are less severe than those I experienced thirty years ago. Typically treatment centers want their clients to get through this quickly and start participating in groups as soon as possible. Family and friends can take comfort in knowing that this is a short phase of the recovery process. Soon it will be over, and the addict will look forward to a healthier body and mind.

If someone you love is going through this withdrawal period at home and you are wondering what to do to help, you may need to speak with their doctor. The doctor will let you know what to watch out for, what may be normal or not. For the most part, this person is not going to want to be around anyone or socialize. Stay sensitive to the person's needs; give them the space and time they need to cycle the drugs out of their system.

> ### *Don't quit.*
> ### *Suffer now and live the rest of your life*
> ### *as a champion.*
> —*Muhammad Ali*

Chapter 21

Getting the Treatment

What do people do all day in treatment?

> " After several calls, I found Valley Hope. It was an answer to our prayers. The next day his dad and I drove Joe to Valley Hope. There was not much talking going on during the ride. [I was relieved to see] it was a very nice place, but I hated to leave him—I knew it was going to be very hard for him."
>
> —*Gladys Herzanek, my mom*

My personal treatment program was, and still is, considered fairly typical. Before I entered treatment, one of the reps met with me and asked about my drug use. He said I had a choice: *I could choose to use, or to not use, drugs and alcohol.* I know this will sound weird to someone who has not struggled with addiction, but up to that moment I don't recall ever thinking of quitting completely. At first, I was just going through the motions, talking with the rep and then agreeing to go to treatment. It was just a way to get my family off my back. I had no great expectations about the success of treatment. At the time, I thought I was just buying myself some time. But the idea of actually quitting seemed to persist in my thinking; the seed was planted that would move me toward recovery.

After that initial meeting, I packed my bag, and my parents dropped me off at Valley Hope in Atchison, Kansas, about sixty miles from my home in Kansas City. For me, this small, seemingly insignificant town in Kansas would become the place that would save my life.

Most people who enter treatment will have been using alcohol or drugs right up to the time they arrive. I was a multi-drug user, so my detox was a bit unpredictable. I was told to expect a few difficult days. They were right. Very shortly after I arrived, I started feeling *out of sorts.* These feelings went from bad to worse. Today treatment centers give people medications to help lessen this painful phase, but not when I went through it.

People going through detox are closely monitored and kept in rooms away from others. With professional staff close by, it re-

> *I was told to expect a few difficult days. They were right.*

ally is the safest place for a user to be. I was the only person in a sparse room with three or four beds and a bathroom. Soon after I arrived, I glanced out the window and saw an ambulance tearing up to the front of the building. *What's going on now? Are they here for me?* The nurse told me that someone had consumed a bottle of aftershave lotion, because it contained about ten-percent alcohol.

I experienced alternating waves of extreme temperature changes, from bone-chilling shivers to excessive sweating. I lay in bed and looked at the ceiling for hours. The nurse came and wrapped me in warm blankets when I was shivering. Once I asked the nurse to open the window; it wasn't hot, but the room had a terrible odor. She opened the window and left. I soon realized that I was the reason for the bad odor—the toxins were leaving my body.

This routine lasted a couple days—cold, then hot, back to chills and so forth—while all sorts of crazy thoughts raced through my mind.

I was paranoid, thinking people on the other side of the wall were talking about me. I thought I would be safer in the bathroom. Once in there, things got worse. I thought the room was starting to get smaller, so I went back to lie on the bed. I was told later that they were seriously considering taking me to the nearest hospital. This difficult period lasted about a week. After that I started sleeping much better. The crazy thoughts subsided, I started to emotionally come out of my shell and I began to get a lot out of the groups I had begun attending. When it warmed up outside we played volleyball on the weekends; this was the first time I'd played a team sport in at least ten years.

A day at a treatment center has regularly scheduled activities—radically different from my previous regularly scheduled activities! For starters, there was breakfast from 7:00 to 8:00 every morning. I wasn't used to eating breakfast until 2 or 3 o'clock in the afternoon, if at all. Food had become a non-essential for me. Over the years it had gotten to the point that eating would just mess up a good high. After breakfast there was a class or lecture. During the next twenty-eight days, I received a crash course on addiction, learning how these substances had affected all the organs of my body, physically and mentally. I learned of all the damage that I may have done to myself, as well as how to reverse it.

I also learned that my problems were not unique. The lectures and classes were great opportunities to get answers to issues I was wondering about. We would break into smaller groups where some good discussions took place. Some of the topics included, *Can life be fun without drugs? What do you do on weekends without drugs? Who will I hang out with?* I was beginning to become more and more involved, and this was something that I hadn't planned on. During my first group meetings, I didn't feel comfortable participating; my hands would sweat, I always sat in the back and it was all I could do to say my name when we introduced ourselves. By the end of my treatment, I had started to contribute to the discussions and I looked forward to going.

Some of the lectures were almost like a spiritual experience. I remember sitting in my chair (one of those classroom chairs with an attached table) listening to a speaker talk about the progression of addiction. I can still picture this guy standing there in a yellow shirt, with a small podium in front of him. He was describing what had happened to *me. How did he know that?* Later, in a small group, I heard others say similar things about what they had been learning. It was as if we had all been tricked by our addictions.

Everyone in treatment is assigned a counselor and a chaplain to meet with for one-on-one sessions. This setting, and the confidentiality that comes with it, allows participants the means to unload deep hurts from the past. It can also be a time to receive more focused, personal attention.

After a few meetings with my counselor, I felt that I could open up to him. During my active using, I had done some foolish things—things I had stuffed and never talked about. I'm not talking about committing the crime of the century, but just stupid, embarrassing, and selfish things. For instance, one day when my former wife Vicki and I got into a shouting match, she became extremely

> *He was describing what had happened to me. "How did he know that?" I learned that my problems were not unique.*

upset and stormed out of the apartment—so fast that she forgot her purse. I took it, dumped the contents on the barbecue grill, doused everything with lighter fluid and set it on fire.

Free Time

I started jogging regularly. I would go for a run, come back, relax, and have a smoke. (Eventually running won out over smoking, and I quit that as well, a couple of years later.)

> *I don't get high, but sometimes I wish I did.*
> *That way, when I messed up in life*
> *I would have an excuse.*
> *But right now there's no rehab for stupidity.*
> —*Chris Rock*

There is something unique about the residential treatment experience that is difficult for me to describe. Being pulled out of the mess I was in, and suddenly dropped into a large group of men and women who had recently experienced the same thing, was strange and surreal—but in a good way. One of the guys I met in treatment had done something similar to what I did when I burned the contents of Vicki's purse on the grill. He and his wife had gone camping, and both of them became very drunk and started arguing. He too, dumped everything from his wife's purse on the fire—only he used a campfire instead of a grill.

Like many other treatment centers, Valley Hope strongly encouraged us to attend AA meetings when we returned home. I knew nothing about AA. The only mental picture I had of these meetings was that of a group of old drunks sitting around drinking coffee and smoking cigarettes. While still in treatment, our group was taken into the town of Atchison once a week to attend an AA meeting. I went, but had no plans to continue going to these meetings after I left treatment. Although some of my memories of these times are foggy, I do remember getting to a place where I actually liked being a part of these meetings.

Cup Hanging

On the last day of treatment, there was a little ceremony called "cup hanging" for those graduating from the program. All along the walls in one big room were coffee cups. Graduates would write something on their cups about their time in treatment. My cup said "Time Keeps on Slippin'," the title of a Steve Miller song. To me, it was a reminder to take life one day at a time. There were four or five of us who hung our cups that day. We were given the opportunity to share some of our experiences with the group, but most of us, including myself, became a bit too choked up to speak. It was a very emotional time for me—a real feeling of accomplishment—the first time in sixteen years that I had gone four weeks without a drink or drug.

Follow-up

Although I was returning home, my treatment wasn't completely over. The last part of my program involved follow-up group work at a local setting in Kansas City, as well as counseling for the initial transition to the outside world. The topics for these groups were a bit different from those in treatment. The people in these groups now had jobs and new responsibilities. These discussions consisted of ways to deal with stress, anger, and anxiety without using drugs or alcohol. I took advantage of this counseling for the next few months. My new counselor, Bob, a Native American about my age and also in recovery, was a laid-back person with a certain peace of mind. I could tell that he wasn't faking it. He enjoyed life without alcohol or drugs—and that was what I wanted. I later found out that he was also a Christian.

Inpatient residential treatment is not always imperative, but if it is economically feasible, it's a great way to begin recovery. Treatment centers generally know how to transform a sick, often angry, hurt, and fearful addict into a new person—full of potential, with a renewed spirit, and the promise of a new life in recovery.

It had taken me years to get into the sad and deplorable state that I was in. I was physically, mentally, emotionally and spiritually bankrupt. I don't believe there is a quick fix for someone like myself. But with the right attitude, prayer, and a caring recovery community "all things are possible."

Chapter 22

Drugs: The Gift That Keeps on Giving

What should I know about hep C?

I debated whether to include this chapter or not. How much do I really want to share? Some parts of my addiction story are still difficult to talk about, even after working in this field for many years. Nevertheless, I know that many people in recovery have had the same complications, so this is why I'm choosing to share this part of my life. Hopefully my experience can be an encouragement to some of you.

I was at the twenty-two-year mark in my sobriety—twenty-two years of complete abstinence from drugs and alcohol. Then, while riding a dirt-bike in Grand Junction, Colorado, I ruptured a disk in my neck and needed surgery. The operation was not all that unusual—take a disk out, and replace it with a piece of bone from my hip. I was at the hospital getting prepped for the operation when a nurse took my surgeon aside. I didn't catch everything, but they were talking about whether to go ahead with the operation. The blood work was showing a problem with my liver function. The surgeon said it shouldn't affect surgery and that "we would deal with that problem later." He didn't appear to be too concerned, but I knew otherwise from the look on the nurse's face.

A couple weeks later I saw my primary care physician. He drew some blood, and told me to come back the next week for the results. He didn't seem too concerned. My health had been great for years prior to this neck problem. I was running regularly and had even competed in races and marathons.

> *I know God will not give me*
> *anything I can't handle.*
> *I just wish that He didn't trust me so much.*
> —*Mother Teresa*

The next week I returned for the results. My doctor of twenty years stood there in his white coat and stethoscope and told me my liver function was out of whack (I'm sure he used more technical jargon). Then he told me I had tested positive for hepatitis C. Time seemed to slow down for just a minute. I didn't know a lot about hep C, but I did know it could be a big deal. I found out later it was something I had been carrying around in my blood for twenty years. I had apparently contracted it during my alcohol- and drug-using years. It is a virus that slowly damages the liver, but symptoms are not evident until it has reached advanced stages—sometimes decades later. For many, this diagnosis can be a sore reminder of their old lives, and personal regrets can come flooding back.

Hepatitis C is not something that is routinely tested for, until the liver begins to function poorly. Hep C is the number one reason for liver transplants, and most people on the transplant waiting list die waiting for a donor.

I met with a liver specialist, a doctor specializing in gastrointestinal problems, who explained my treatment options to me. I was about to begin taking a host of new drugs in an attempt to kill the virus. A promising new hep C-fighting drug was to be released in a few months. So what do we do in the meantime? Take the kids and go to Disney World, of course! My neck was healed by then, and there were still no real symptoms of the hep C, so off we went.

There was no plan B. My choices were either treatment or liver failure. Treatment lasted about a year and required weekly injections of a drug called Interferon as well as many other pills. I was told that a large number of people who undergo this treatment become severely depressed—often suicidal. Because of this potential depression, it was strongly encouraged that I take an anti-depressant. So I did.

Looking back on my treatment, I know that I would have *had* to take the anti-depressant anyway, because my ordeal was beyond difficult. You are most likely familiar with the information sheet that is attached with any prescription, listing all the possible side effects. I believe I may have experienced them all—guess I'm just a lucky guy! (I should mention that this is not always the case; I've spoken to several others who did not experience side effects nearly as severe as mine when they went through hep C treatment.) That year was a rollercoaster for my family and me. There were days when I could not get out of bed, and I would isolate myself from everyone. Toward the end of my treatment I was very thin and weak, having lost over forty pounds, and couldn't make it up a flight of steps without stopping to rest. My mental state was unpredictable and my hearing was very sensitive to certain sounds; there was a constant ringing in my ears.

"Living with someone going through treatment for hep C is not easy. During that year, the kids and I learned to tolerate and adjust to a life of unpredictability. Joe became reclusive, shutting us off from himself physically and mentally. He would put a "Do Not Disturb" sign on the basement door and stay down there for days—coming up a couple times during the day when no one was around, and going right back. There was even a time that I raced home from work one afternoon to make sure that he was still alive. I knew he was dangerously depressed, and I hadn't been able to reach him on the phone all day. It turned out that he just didn't want to talk to anyone. One time he left for four days and never told us where he was going. Later, after he returned, we found out that he had gone to a local hotel where he could have complete silence and seclusion.

"Joe became very sensitive to sound at times. He would become very annoyed by the slightest noise, such as someone playing pool in the basement when he was upstairs in the living room.

"This all happened at a time when we were dealing with teenage rebellion issues with Jake. It was not an easy time for us. I wish there had been some kind of hep C support group for families—to help prepare us for, and provide us with support during these trying times. I know that other families are going to need help. Hep C cases are supposed to triple over the next decade."

—*Judy Herzanek*

The good news is that my treatment was successful: all tests continue to indicate that the virus is gone. My treatment for hep C ended ten years ago, and I'm grateful to be writing this today. But I haven't been able to get off the anti-depressant. I made two calculated attempts, under my doctor's guidance, but each attempt left me feeling very uncomfortable and more miserable. So what does that mean? I think it means that my brain, my central nervous system, has become chemically dependent on the drug. Part of me does not like taking it. I've come to believe that the fewer substances a person has in their system, the better. Just the same, this particular drug seems to have a negative effect only when I stop taking it. Otherwise, I would say that with the help of this medication, I feel pretty normal. So what's a person to do? For me, I've accepted that I will continue to take it from now on. I don't increase the dose, so I don't build up a tolerance to it. And, life is good.

My purpose for including this story is twofold. First, I want people to know that hep C is treatable, and that the new medications for treating it are very effective. In fact, people can get rid of the virus up to eighty percent of the time. My liver function is completely normal now. Second, I want families to be aware of some of the obstacles and decisions they may face upon learning that a loved one has hepatitis C. A recovering person will find himself needing different types of drugs throughout his lifetime, and it is important to discuss options thoroughly with a physician. Honestly discussing the past will ensure the safety of the person in recovery, avoiding any dangers of future addiction problems. A doctor will explain which drugs to avoid and which are safe. Having to take or continuing to take an anti-depressant is not something a user should dread or feel bad about. If someone makes a genuine attempt, with the help of his physician, to discontinue use of an anti-depressant drug and finds that they can't function without it, just be assured that this is okay.

These medications are available to improve and maintain a person's quality of life. A clean and sober person who needs to take an anti-depressant is in much better condition than when they were using.

> *When you can't solve the problem, manage it.*
> —*Robert H. Schuller*

Chapter 23
Least Likely to Succeed

What are alternative treatments for recovery, and do they work?

What is meant by *alternative* treatment? This refers to an alternative to what appears to be the standard or most effective treatment. Some are controversial and will not be helpful for everyone.

Diet

One alternative is a change in diet. Some people believe that eating certain foods and vitamins may help them to end their addiction. I do believe that good nutrition plays an important role in recovery. Our bodies need nutritious food, exercise, and proper rest. Certain foods may even help alleviate some of the craving. Can they help one to facilitate recovery? Absolutely. But will nutrition, a special diet, or supplements end addiction and ensure successful recovery? I don't think so.

> *So many roads. So many detours.*
> *So many choices. So many mistakes.*
> —*Sarah Jessica Parker*

Acupuncture

Acupuncture is another treatment that can offer some positive results. For anyone not familiar with acupuncture, it is an Eastern treatment in which small needles are used to pierce the body at points where the flow of energy is thought to be blocked. The end result is supposed to restore energetic balance and create improved organ function. Clinical studies of this treatment are unable to verify positive results for ending addiction, although it does appear to offer some relief for a few people.

Saunas and Vitamins

As wonderful as saunas and vitamins may be, to help you feel good (at least in the short term), they will not cure addiction. There are a few groups that would like you to believe otherwise.

Ibogaine

Ibogaine treatment is another option that has yet to be proven to work. Ibogaine comes from an African plant that when ingested causes a hallucinogenic effect similar to peyote, an herb that some Native Americans use in spiritual ceremonies. Ibogaine has long been used in shamanic rituals of initiation and spiritual quests. It is said to *help cure addictions of all kinds.* However, some people have found using Ibogaine to be a terrifying experience. The FDA has not approved this drug, so it is illegal in the United States, but one can find it being used in clinics in Mexico.

> ### *There's too much confusion, I can't get no relief.*
> —Jimi Hendrix, *All Along the Watchtower*

Meditation

One more popular alternative is the practice of meditation. Meditation can mean different things to different people. Some see it as part of their religious experience. To sit, be still, and take a mental break from our fast-paced lives is a good idea for anyone. Time to stop and reflect on what's really important can help people make better life choices. Is it going to end addiction for the person who has spent years or decades consumed with drugs and alcohol? Not likely. Will it convince the hardcore meth or heroin addict to abstain from using? Don't count on it. However, it may very well be a healthy activity for a person in recovery.

I believe our prayer life can be similar to a two-way conversation with God. We pray and then we listen.

> ## Be still and know that I am God . . .
> —*Psalm 46:10*

Televangelism

Some might even consider late-night religious programming as an alternative treatment. Certain TV personalities would like you to think so. You may have clicked onto a program where a televangelist is promising a miracle healing. Often this *healing* will require sending a "love offering" to the host of the show. Can God do miracles still today? I believe He can and does, but are you going to get your miracle cure over the airwaves? Don't count on it. Finding a local faith community to attend would be much more beneficial.

Other Alternatives

There are other alternatives, from yoga, amino acid drips, hypnosis, art therapy, psychodrama, equine therapy, guided meditation—to subscribing to an online self-recovery system—even blogging your way toward recovery. However, I think you probably get the gist of what I want to emphasize in this chapter: Be wary of *quick-fix* gimmicks that promise an easy recovery. In fact, I would suggest that you be very leery of anyone claiming to have a cure or anyone who even uses the words "cure" and "addiction" in the same sentence. Those who claim these "treatments" to be a cure are either uninformed or have something to sell you. Recovery is going to take time and effort. Being successful at anything worthwhile requires commitment and persistence.

> *There are no shortcuts to restoring a life.*

The most effective form of treatment is a combination of education about addiction and what people in recovery call "talk therapy" (conversations with groups, counselors, and others in varying stages of recovery). Most if not all of the alternative solutions mentioned above do not focus on either of these two components.

Families and concerned friends should be aware that none of these alternative remedies will result in recovery if they are used as "stand alone" treatments. However, having said that—when combined with education, prayer and talk therapy, some may be helpful.

> *History teaches us that men ... behave wisely once they have exhausted all other alternatives.*
>
> —*Abba Eban*

I know a young woman, Megan, who tried a combination of exercise and nutrition for years. After several relapses, she finally started attending some recovery groups and getting counseling. She has now been sober for over five years. Nutrition and exercise are still a big part of her life. However, having a support group and some friends in recovery has been the key to her success. She admitted to me later that her fear of people kept her away from what she now knows she needed the most.

Often, a friend or family member will tell me that a dependent person they know has already tried a certain recovery group, but didn't like going. But my answer will often be, "So what?" Life sometimes requires that we do things we don't like to do. Alcoholics or addicts are not always the best ones to decide what is the most effective treatment program for them. They are where they are because their decision-making process has malfunctioned. Now may be the time for someone else to tell them what's best for them, even if it involves a long-term commitment to something they may, at first, find unpleasant. There are no shortcuts to restoring a life.

> *Rarely have we seen a person fail*
> *who has thoroughly followed our path.*
> *Those who do not recover*
> *are people who cannot or will not*
> *completely give themselves*
> *to this simple program*
> —*Chapter 5, AA Big Book, How it Works*

Part 3 Overview:
Key Points to Remember

- Many different forms of treatment exist:
  - *counseling*
  - *groups*
  - *outpatient care*
  - *intensive outpatient care*
  - *inpatient/residential care*
  - *gender-specific groups*
  - *twelve-step groups*

- Ask about discounts on treatment.

- Recovering people need other recovering people, and twelve-step groups are very beneficial.

- People do not have to hit *rock bottom*. When possible, *raise their bottom.*

- Pain can be a wonderful teacher.

- Do not rob someone of natural consequences.

- Recovery rates from meth addiction are about the same as for other drugs.

- Withdrawal from drugs is psychological as well as physical. Symptoms are the opposite of what the drug's effects were.

- Hepatitis C can be in a person's body for decades without being detected. New treatments for hep C can be very effective.

- There are no shortcuts to recovery.

.Life
in
Recovery

Chapter 24

A Whole New World

What exactly is recovery?

People like me who experience the recovery process are on an *adventure*—difficult and challenging at times, with no certain destination. It's a real life-long quest. I like to say that life is an odyssey, an extended adventure with peaks and valleys. A person in recovery can use this time to find greater life purpose and be healthy enough to help others fight the battle of addiction. This is a great way to think about life in recovery.

> "After he went through treatment and began recovery, he became a handsome man with a big smile. These times were very difficult for Joe and our family. I believe this has made a much stronger man out of Joe, and I am very proud of him. I think it's so sad to see so many people using drugs and they may not get the chance that Joe did. [Seeing what love and support can do over the years,] my hope is now for every addict to have someone who loves them and won't give up on them.
>
> "After Joe was well into recovery, I no longer had to check the paper every morning to see if he had been in a drug bust. I didn't have to pray every time I heard a siren,

> wondering if he had an accident or overdose. His recovery
> was a true blessing not only for him, but for me as well."
> —*Gladys Herzanek*

The first part of recovery is one of restoring and rebuilding all the damage that has been done. Family members are still vulnerable and are slowly learning how to trust the addict again. It takes time before everyone involved begins to feel better. For the first time, the recovering person starts to realize that the real world is not such a bad place after all, and that there are plenty of people willing to help them through this process.

Those in recovery soon begin to feel better physically and mentally, and their attitude toward life radically transforms. Making amends to some of the people who have been harmed brings peace as well. The first year or so is a little awkward. They are experiencing life in its fullest—both the highs and the lows. The journey has only begun, and they are starting to enjoy the trip.

In recovery, time is a big deal. Time provides strength and signals progress. The longer a person abstains, the stronger they become. The daily effort the recovering person makes is essential for long-term success. I know personally that it takes time to prove to family and friends that you really have changed, and to rebuild trust. Before my recovery, I used to spend virtually all my waking hours feeding my addiction. It became exhausting. By comparison, focusing on my recovery now requires only an hour or two a day. Reading, praying, going to a group, or exercising are small prices to pay for my new life. I have developed strong, healthy friendships—real friendships with people who genuinely care about me, who want what's best for me, and who will listen and tell me when I'm making mistakes.

Real work, which I liked to avoid while using, was not as bad as I had once thought. I soon realized that it was actually possible to do something I enjoyed and get paid for it. Now, over thirty years later, what once consumed my life—alcohol and drugs—no longer controls me. In fact, it's almost as though that whole nightmare of my past happened to someone else. My high school senior class would have voted me "Most Likely to End up in Jail." I eventually did end up in jail, but it has been for sixteen years as a chaplain and substance abuse counselor!

My time in recovery has taken me places I never dreamed of. I enjoy work that is meaningful and have a strong marriage, a great family, and friends. I'm blessed to be able to live near the Rocky Mountains of Colorado, which I often hike and climb. I sleep at night. My future looks good, not bleak.

> *In recovery, time is a big deal. Time equals strength and signals progress.*

But it hasn't always been fun. Recovery has been grueling at times, but going back to my old way of life would have been much worse. Painful and stressful times will come—and they also will pass. Every challenge makes us stronger.

One of the rewards of my recovery is experiencing a renewed relationship with my daughter and former wife. Our past life together was the pits. My substance use inflicted tremendous harm on both of these relationships. The lying, angry outbursts, broken promises, and jealous rages were ugly. After saying "I'm sorry" about ten thousand times, I decided to just stop saying it. *Even I* didn't believe me. I've included some of their personal testimony throughout the book to share with you the real-life drama surrounding the problem of addiction. The impact is great, but families experiencing the devastation of alcohol and drug abuse can all press on in the recovery stage toward reconciliation. I've heard it said that if someone has a hundred problems, and one of them is addiction, then they really only have one problem. After I faced my addiction and dealt with it accordingly, many of these other issues began to fade away.

All of what my family endured is in the past now, and we get along great. Vicki, my former wife, and our daughter, Jami, along with my wife Judy and our two kids, Jake and Jess, have all grown to enjoy each other's company. Over time, Vicki and Judy have become girlfriends. It may be difficult to believe, but we even go on vacations together! Christmas, Thanksgiving, and other holidays are now enjoyed rather than dreaded. Really, I'm not making this up.

> "I remember seeing Joe shortly after he came out [of treatment] and I truly believed he could not do it. Today I am proud of the man Joe has become. He has restored his relationship with Jami and included me in his life with his current family. Without his recovery experience, I would not have become the woman I am today. I knew nothing about recovery when he entered treatment.
>
> " . . . recovery allows divorced individuals to live peacefully with our pasts through forgiveness and acceptance. I am grateful we have that kind of relationship."
>
> —*Vicki, my former wife*

There is a lot to celebrate and look forward to each day, now that I'm not enslaved to an addiction. I'm no longer at war with myself, my family, or the world. None of this happened overnight, and it certainly wasn't a trouble-free recovery period. But the end result has been worth it all.

Chapter 25
Whole Person Recovery: The Mind

Can the mind be healed?

> ### I'm Not Crazy, I'm Just A Little Unwell
> —Matchbox 20: *Unwell*

Mind: *the human consciousness that originates in the brain and is manifested in thought, memory, perception, feeling, will, or imagination.* —**Webster's Dictionary**

Alcohol and drugs affect the brain more than any other vital organ. It is with the use of our brain that we make judgments and decisions, calculate risks, develop attitudes, learn new skills, and so much more. When we talk about substance use and abuse, we are talking about mind-altering chemicals that travel into the bloodstream and then to the brain.

We have already discussed the different categories of drugs, their effects, and why some people choose one type over another. While under the influence of mind-altering drugs, people engage in high-risk behaviors and do things they might not do otherwise.

"What I do remember about my Dad during those days, strangely, are these stories—scary events that happened, things that today I am amazed I actually lived through. But I loved my Dad—he could do no wrong. He was perfect in my eyes; he was what I wanted most—to have a dad. And because I could only have him when it was convenient for him, made our time more special . . . he was my hero and to be with him was the best thing in the world.

"I remember flying in a plane with my Dad and his friend—a small two-seater plane and we would fly way up high. Then they would turn off the engine, and we would fall almost to the ground. I saw a telephone pole up close! It was SO MUCH FUN! . . . Dad was always fun to me.

"I remember him bringing me a fur coat and jewelry from Mexico. He was my hero. I got teased so much at school for having a fur coat [but I didn't care]. I loved it, because it came from my Dad!! He was the one who made me the happiest.

"I remember staying with my Dad at one of his houses. Someone had stolen a lot of money from him and no one was allowed to leave. His friend, Steve, was holding a machine gun at the door. Dad's girlfriend, Rose, was trying to keep everything calm . . . I was calm, I just wanted something to eat. He was my Dad, and to me there was nothing wrong or strange about any of what was happening! My friend Krista's mom came . . . and took me away. He was still my hero."

—Jami, my daughter

Continued use over long periods of time can greatly distort the normal thinking process. It can even alter the sound thinking of family members. For me, when I was using, there was a significant change in my attitude. Drug and chemical abuse was affecting the chemical balance in my brain. It was making me very negative toward people and life in general—narcissistic as well. Other people's feelings were their problem. Being honest became less and less important; I could look a person in the eye and make up any excuse, or lie on the spot, if it suited my needs.

I've heard the brain described as an orchestra performing a symphony. When a couple of "instruments" stop, or play off-key, it changes everything. At first the music may just sound funny. After a while it can get very confusing. People do crazy things and think some crazy thoughts when they are under the influence. I know that I did.

> ### *Being sober on a bus is, like, totally different than being drunk on a bus.*
> —*Ozzy Osbourne*

Our thoughts affect everything in our lives—from what shoes to put on in the morning, to what career we choose, or whom we marry. What unfolds in the course of our lives starts with our thoughts. Every action we carry out and every word we say begins as an idea or impression in our brain. It's all about our thoughts.

So after people stop using drugs and alcohol, how do they begin to heal their minds? How do they change their thoughts and mentally *feel better?* A good place to start is by acknowledging that a problem exists and becoming convinced that there is a solution. Long periods of addiction skew people's thoughts. They need to adjust the way they view themselves and others. They need to remind themselves that they are *not crazy* and that they need help from other people. Having some kind of support group and talk therapy is critical for this part of recovery. People don't need help taking a multiple vitamin or going for a walk, but they do need help to heal their minds.

> *It takes but one positive thought when given a chance to survive and thrive to overpower an entire army of negative thoughts.*
>
> —*Robert H. Schuller*

Reading about recovery, engaging in exercise, and learning about nutrition are great ways to gain new knowledge. But when it comes to healing the mind, recovering addicts need like-minded people around, encouraging them to stay focused. In this phase of recovery, community is essential—people who will offer hope when things look difficult. When one friend in recovery is weak, there are others to cheer him on, to help him to keep moving forward and to stay strong.

Groups

Group therapy is very powerful. That is why there is so much of it taking place. (There is actually a bar in my neighborhood called *Group Therapy*.) People learn from one another; they take what they've heard from another recovering person and apply it to their new lives. The recovering person learns from these experiences, and in turn shares his triumphs and downfalls with others. Often, someone will approach me after a meeting and say, "I'm glad I came tonight. What you said was exactly what I needed to hear." You can't buy moments like this. The reverse happens to me as well when I hear encouraging words from someone at a meeting.

Counseling

One-on-one counseling is also vital. I took advantage of recovery groups and professional counseling—I needed both. Meetings and support groups, AA groups, a therapist, sponsor or mentor—all help to make recovery possible. No one recovers alone. The mass of tissue inside our skull called a brain will get healthier with nutrition and exercise, but our thoughts are a different story: they are what got us into this mess in the first place. Changing the way we think also means getting help from those who understand addiction—listening to others who have recovered and/or professionals who specialize in this field. This is why someone in recovery needs help from other people besides family members, who may not be able to relate to issues the addict is dealing with.

Prayer

Prayer played a big role in my recovery as well. It's been said that we should pray like it all depends on God and work like it all depends on us.

Reading

When I was addicted, reading seemed boring. The only thing I read was an occasional newspaper article. But during recovery, I started to read all the books I could find on addiction and recovery—three or four books a week on every aspect of getting well. I didn't own a TV, I was single and I suddenly found myself with a lot of extra time. I quickly became a fast reader.

Act on Advice

After getting some wise counsel, both from others and through books, a person then needs to act—to follow some of the advice they have received. My own thinking was about as mixed up as it could get. Sixteen years of drug abuse had created a tangled web of distorted thinking. All my insecurity, fear and mistrust, along with a completely negative attitude toward life and people, took time to change. Now, I would say that my thought processes are back to normal (or at least vastly improved—not sure if my wife would agree with this statement).

Maintenance

Continued maintenance is crucial for everyone in recovery, to ensure that they don't return to their old way of thinking. This is why I continue to attend, and also lead, twelve-step meetings. Also, counseling others and helping them to recover is like therapy for me; It's one of the best ways for me to stay mentally healthy. Part of healing the mind is acting on the desire to live for more than your own selfish desires. Most abusers have lived out many days just thinking about themselves. Encourage your recovering loved one to help someone else who may be struggling. They might be amazed to see how much they have to offer!

Chapter 26
Whole Person Recovery: The Body

What roles do nutrition and exercise play in recovery?

Healing the whole person is the ultimate goal of recovery. Addiction to any substance causes damage to every area of life. The body suffers as well as the mind and spirit. One of the most amazing things to me is the body's ability to heal itself. Years or even decades of misuse and abuse can often be reversed. I've seen this happen both with myself and with many other recovering people as well.

Drug abuse and addiction can be compared to constantly beating ourselves up with a baseball bat. Over time, we can start to look and feel pretty bad. Depriving our bodies of basic nutrition, adequate water, proper sleep and exercise, is a bad idea, whether you are an addict or not. But for substance abusers, the ill-effects are multiplied. During the course of their addiction, abusers will remove all the necessary nutrients from their body and replace them with large amounts of alcohol and drugs. This is similar to a hiker who is attempting to climb a mountain carrying a backpack full of rocks.

So when a person quits using and begins recovery, getting rid of the rocks—those unnecessary hindrances—will have immediate, positive results on the body, both on the outside as well as the inside. In a few months, a person will start to see years or decades of physical problems begin to improve. Phase one of healing the body is to stop poisoning it.

Nutrition

Large quantities of alcohol are obviously harmful to the body. After stopping the bad stuff from entering the bloodstream, the toxins need to be replaced with good basic nutrition. The Lord only knows how many deadly toxins were flowing through my veins from the street drugs that I consumed. I mentioned that I am not a doctor; I am also not a certified nutritionist. But I have studied this topic a great deal over the years. During my training to become a certified addiction counselor, I was required to take classes on nutrition and pharmacology. Most recovering people become involved in health and nutrition on their own. People who, prior to recovery, paid very little attention to diet and exercise, find themselves

> ### *You've got bad eating habits if you use a grocery cart in 7-Eleven.*
> —*Dennis Miller*

reading all they can on the topic. After all, an interest in good health is a normal progression as the person searches for new ways to heal and feel better. This is a great idea, but let me provide a word of caution. Eating good food, taking vitamin and mineral supplements, and engaging in some exercise, is important. But finding that *miracle-missing nutrient* that will give you a magical sense of well-being isn't going to happen. It is important to mention this for two reasons: First of all, I've been down that dead-end road. I tried to find that miracle supplement myself for years with no results. I spent a lot of time researching nutrition and supplementation. Part of me wanted to know how to stay healthy and fit; I wanted to feel better. Another part of me was secretly looking for that *one missing nutrient* that would create a dramatic change. I tried several dozen products over the years, including bee pollen, DHEA, flaxseed oil, amino acids, herbs and Guarana. All of these may be good for you, but for me, they didn't have any dramatic or immediate effects. Like many recovering addicts, I wanted a quick cure. Today I continue to take vitamin and mineral supplements, because I believe they are good for my body in the long run, but I've stopped looking for the silver bullet.

My second caution is that you will encounter well-meaning people who will try to convince you that such a supplement *does* exist. It doesn't; you can stop looking. Don't waste your time and money. There is nothing new about the fact that with proper nutrition the body really does heal itself, and this is the real miracle! Some improvements may be noticeable right away, but just like addiction, recovery is a process for the body that takes time.

There are numerous studies and volumes written on the topic of nutrition (see "Nutrition" in the Resources section of this book). After much reading, trying the latest foods, diets, and supplements, I have come to believe that the basics haven't changed much over the years. What has changed is the mass production of fast foods with little to no nutritional value. Foods high in fat, sugar, caffeine—and with names of ingredients that we can't even pronounce—should be avoided. Eating well helps the body and brain to repair. Fresh fruits, vegetables, whole grains, fish, lean meat, and yogurt, are all good for a recovering person. Almost anything a person can buy at a fast food restaurant isn't. The public's knowledge of and interest in food and nutrition is growing exponentially. Evidence of this is the rapid growth of the natural foods industry, with such stores as Whole Foods. Healthy eating—purchasing foods high in nutritional value and low in harmful additives—may cost a little more, but in the long run, it's worth it.

Exercise

Exercise is not a four-letter word. Our bodies were meant to move. American society, with all of its conveniences, does not require much physical activity. Food can be delivered to your door now, and the work-place often requires employees to spend most of their working hours sitting at a desk. We now drive or ride to most places. We are a sedentary society. I've heard it said that we have become a nation of *watchers.*

This is not good for anyone's body—especially that of a recovering person. Even short walks can pay big dividends for mental and physical health. Schools are now reinstating exercise programs for children, as child obesity has become a serious problem. Somewhere in our quest for technological advancement, we have forgotten some basics about good health.

I strongly suggest that all recovering people exercise on a regular basis. The choices are many and varied—from walking, biking, and swimming, to running marathons. It is not difficult for a person to find something that they like (or hate the least) and start doing it. Many recovering people will find themselves surprised and impressed with the results, once they begin. Often recovering people will channel time and energy that they previously spent on drug use to fuel their newfound passion—physical exercise.

> *Everybody needs a way out of that pain.*
> *Many people choose drugs and alcohol.*
> *Some people obsessively exercise or develop*
> *strange dietary habits, which is what I did.*
> *At least it got me toward a path of healthier living.*
>
> —*Mariel Hemingway*

What worked for me was running. I started with a mile or two each day. I can't say it was a lot of fun in the beginning, but I grew to like it. Running was a way for me to handle the stress and frustration I experienced during early recovery. After a while, I was hooked. Vigorous aerobic exercise of some kind has been proven to produce natural feel-good chemicals in the body. Still, today, I continue to exercise regularly. Running may not be for everyone, but a recovering person needs to find something that works. Exercise and good nutritional choices can be the start of a whole new healthy lifestyle. Make sure you take time to encourage your recovering loved one to watch their diet and to begin some kind of physical activity.

Chapter 27

Whole Person Recovery: The Spirit

Do we have to talk about religion?

We see the roadside signs all the time: "Rockville Wine and Spirits"; "Kelly's Wine and Spirits"; "Horizon Wine and Spirits." What is a *spirit?* What message are these stores trying to convey?

We've talked about recovery being for the whole person. So far we have covered mind and body. The third aspect, the spirit, is equal in importance, but the most difficult to explain. So, what exactly do we mean by *spiritual recovery?* Is it about religion? Is it the same for everyone?

My Search

For me, this has been a long but fulfilling search. When I began my recovery from wine, *spirits,* and other drugs, I had no idea what I was doing. I knew I wanted life to get better. Up until I was in recovery, I thought of spiritual things as part of some religion that wasn't for me. Earlier in life, I had all the religion I needed, which was mostly a negative experience. At the same time, I did want some serenity and peace of mind to go along with my newfound sobriety. And so, my search began.

It took time to get over my preconceived ideas about spiritual matters. At the time, all my thoughts of God were negative. I had no interest in things relating to God. Still, I needed an answer about the *spiritual part* of recovery.

AA and NA refer to a *higher power* or to *God, as I understand him.*

This concept wasn't enough to satisfy the void I was feeling, although it did crack the door open a little to start my spiritual search. This new path of personal growth in recovery sent me on a quest for answers.

My background didn't help. All of my relatives were Catholic. I attended a Catholic parochial school through my elementary school years. Every school day started with mass, during which Sister Ralph often whacked me in the back of the head for talking. Queen of the Holy Rosary Church and my elementary school experience do not bring back fond memories of a *higher power.* Add going to Sunday mass with my parents, and I was attending church six days a week. My first encounters with God were not positive. I couldn't wait to stop going. And I did stop, at about age twelve or thirteen. I left the church thinking that I was facing a long time in purgatory, if not worse.

Thankfully, by the time I began my recovery, much time had passed since then. Both counselors and recovery groups were talking about a *different kind of God,* which encouraged me to seek a different spiritual experience than I had known in my childhood. I was open-minded, and the thought of a kind, benevolent God, a God who genuinely wanted to help me enjoy life, was worth pursuing. And so, the search was on. I read a lot, tried attending several different churches, and explored various religions. This went on for three years.

My new job involved traveling all over the country. I kept a journal for my newfound exercise—running. At the end of one year, when I re-read my journal, I saw that I had traveled to twenty-six different states. This had allowed me to attend different churches all over the country. I tried just about everything: the Crystal Cathedral, a Mormon church in Salt Lake City, the Unity Church in Kansas City, Methodist, Southern Baptist, Buddhist, transcendental meditation—you name it, and I probably gave it a shot.

The old adage says, *analysis can lead to paralysis.* Was this *spirit-being* trying to hide from me? I felt that I was getting closer, but still wasn't sure who I thought God really was. At this point in my quest, I was meditating, and reading different daily devotionals, every morning. (One in particular was a book from AA called *Twenty-Four Hours a Day.*)

> *Separated, I cut myself clean*
> *From a past that comes back*
> *in my darkest of dreams*
> *Been apprehended by a spiritual force*
> *And a grace that replaced*
> *all the me I've divorced*
>
> *I saw a man with a tat on his big fat belly*
> *It wiggled around like marmalade jelly*
> *It took me a while to catch what it said*
> *Cause I had to match the rhythm*
> *Of his belly with my head*
>
> *Jesus saves is what it raved*
> *in a typical tattoo green*
> *He stood on a box in the middle of the city*
> *And claimed he had a dream*
>
> —dc talk, *Jesus Freak*
> (Used by permission of musicservices.org)

After all the searching, a leap of faith was required. A leap of faith is always required. I had "done my homework," asked questions, listened, and prayed for guidance. My committment, my decision was a "matter of fact, this makes the most sense to me" decision. I now have, along with my twelve-step group, another supportive group to encourage me on life's journey. Finding a benevolent God who wants the best for us brings serenity and peace of mind. I'm sharing what worked for me— my personal experience. My leap of faith was to Christianity.

I continue to study the Christian faith, and I have also learned not to make judgments by what I see on television or hear on the news, but to find answers from the Bible and leaders I respect, and my local faith community.

The last thing I want to do in this section is to get too *preachy*. Spiritual growth is very personal. What I'm saying is that spirituality is a big part of recovery and is too important to ignore. Most recovering people will acknowledge that healing involves body, mind, and spirit. I'm thankful that I now have a personal relationship with Christ and to know that my future with God is secure. He has brought me this far, and I'm confident He will carry me the rest of the way.

WINE INTO WATER

You've heard a multitude of prayers on my behalf
I pray that one more is not too much to ask
I've tried to fight this battle by myself
But it's a war that I can't win without your help

So many times I've hurt the ones I love
I pushed them to the edge of giving up
They've stood by me but how much can they stand
If I don't put this bottle in your hands

I shook my fist at heaven
for all the hell that I've been through
Now I'm beggin' for forgiveness
and a miracle from you, cause

Chorus:
To-night I'm as low as any man can go
I'm down and I can't fall much farther
And once upon a time you turned
the water into wine
Now on my knees I'm turning to you father
Could you help me turn the wine back into water

—T. Graham Brown

Chapter 28

Pill for Pill

Is it okay to take medications in recovery?

Medications Used for Recovery

There are a few medications available today that help some people with the initial quitting phase. However, I strongly advise anyone in recovery to consult with a trusted doctor before taking anything. Some medications may help ease withdrawal. I'm talking here about physical withdrawal. One of the more difficult groups of substances for an addict to stop using is pain medications—mainly, the opiate drugs like Vicodin, Percocet, heroin, and OxyContin—because these types of drugs cause a strong physical and psychological dependency. Some medications have been found to help ease the craving for these types of opiates. Similar prescriptions could help with withdrawal from other classes of abused drugs as well. These are not miracle cures, just drugs that may be helpful early in recovery, to be used for a *short period of time.*

The one drug that surprisingly is the most dangerous to stop using after long periods of dependency is alcohol. The sudden withdrawal of alcohol from the body is known to cause seizures. In a detox center, these patients are closely monitored. Stopping the use of tranquilizers like Valium and Xanax can be equally problematic. By comparison, a person withdrawing from heroin does not require the same close supervision. Although painful, quitting the use of heroin rarely causes seizures or death.

> *To cease smoking is the easiest thing I ever did.*
> *I ought to know*
> *because I've done it a thousand times.*
> —*Mark Twain*

Smoking During Recovery

One other drug that I haven't discussed at length is nicotine. Smoking, or using tobacco products, is one of the toughest addictions to stop. Let me say right up front that quitting smoking is *not* the number one concern for the alcoholic or drug addict. If a person is a smoker and is not ready to give that up, don't worry about it—at least for now.

I smoked through the first year or so of my recovery. The thought of quitting everything at once was too much for me, as it is for most people. Even so, addicts do need to realize that nicotine is very harmful to their health and extremely addictive.

According to the American Lung Association, there are currently 48 million Americans (22.9% of adults) addicted to tobacco products. Most of them will say that they wish they could quit. I had been smoking a couple packs of cigarettes each day for over ten years. After making several attempts to quit smoking, and experiencing several relapses, I finally made myself go through a week of hell. After that rough first week, it became easier. Today, over twenty-five years later, the thought of smoking never comes to mind. In fact, I am extremely sensitive—almost to the point of allergic—to the smell of cigarette smoke. I mention nicotine addiction because a very high percentage of people with drug problems are smokers as well.

Taking Drugs During Recovery

In general, a physician knowledgeable about addiction needs to monitor the recovering person's use of medications. I often hear stories of relapse because someone has taken pain medications. The question then is, *What does a person do when they truly need this kind of medication?* What should you do if the addict in your life needs pain medication for surgery, a broken bone, or recovery from oral surgery? I've talked about my own struggle with these same questions when I faced hepatitis C. Here, I want to address this dilemma a little more specifically. How does a recovering addict take drugs like this without bringing their disease out of remission? Well, very cautiously!

I have had a few surgeries over the years, so the issue has come about at different stages of my own recovery. Earlier, I mentioned my neck surgery and the dirt-bike accident. Dirt-bike riding in the mountains is a young man's sport. I thought this might be one of those bonding things a father could do with his son. Instead, it brought about the dilemma of how an addict can use again for valid medical reasons.

After surgery, my doctor wrote a prescription for Percocet, a strong opiate painkiller. I was in a lot of pain, and I was going to continue hurting for at least a few days. My doctor knew that I was a former drug abuser. I had informed him so he could be aware of my tendency to want to keep taking these drugs even after the pain was gone. For the first time in my life, I made sure to take the medications *exactly* as my doctor told me to. The next important thing I did was throw away whatever was left once the pain was gone. It is always a bad idea to save leftover medications.

Some recovering people may even have a chronic pain problem that they have to deal with. But there are many different ways to manage even chronic pain (see "Pain Management" in the Resource section). Opiate-type pain medications like Vicodin, Percocet, and OxyContin are *not* the solutions. Here's why.

Over time, our bodies will build up tolerance to opiate drugs. This can result in an addict taking a large number of pills and becoming dependent on them. It may get to a point where the pills are not working anymore, yet the person keeps taking them for fear of going through withdrawal. The cycle begins all over again. When someone in recovery needs to take pain medication for a legitimate reason, they need to let someone (like another person in recovery) know. It's not difficult to get a refill on most prescriptions. If doctors don't know a person is in recovery, they will assume that the request for a refill is legitimate. But the person in recovery, or their friend or family member, should be sure to tell the doctor of any history of drug use. Following that, the medication should be used as directed for a short period of time, and the remaining pills should be flushed.

> *We are made wise not by*
> *the recollection of our past,*
> *but by the responsibility for our future.*
> —George Bernard Shaw

Stay On Guard

As your loved one continues life in recovery, you should be aware of situations that will naturally present opportunities to use again. Even if twenty years have passed, do not assume a prescription drug won't be a temptation. This kind of event can often disguise itself as a legitimate excuse to *use*. Play an active role in the recovering person's life. Take time to talk through their medical needs with the doctor. No matter how many years have passed, your loved one still needs your support and concern.

Do not assume a prescription drug won't be a temptation.

Chapter 29
Serotonin Rising

How should you deal with depression in recovery?

Years and even decades of alcoholism or drug addiction can do a lot of harm to the body and mind (after all, it is a brain disease). For those of us in recovery, we often see most or all of this damage reversed in a much shorter time period. Proper nutrition, exercise, and counseling can help to accelerate this process even more.

But for some, this will not bring back peace of mind. Even those with a strong faith and mature spiritual life may still battle with depression. In society today, depression is a growing problem. The same is true for some of us in recovery. I want to talk about this because of what I see happening with some recovering men and women. It is frustrating to watch someone doing everything right, yet still not have much joy in life.

Serotonin is the chemical in the brain that helps to stabilize our mood and produces melatonin, which helps us to sleep well. Years of substance abuse seem to affect the brain's ability to produce enough serotonin. There are a host of other reasons one may have low serotonin levels, but the bottom line is this: low levels of serotonin may contribute to depression, and the suffering that results can complicate the already difficult road to recovery. Sometimes family and friends aren't aware of this and can be insensitive to it. People may feel that the recovering person is still unable to care about others and that the depression is a product of still being self-absorbed. This may not be the case at all.

Clinical Depression

The depression I'm talking about is clinical depression—not just being sad. Clinical depression persists for weeks or months. As a concerned party, you may want to look for significant bouts of severe lows. Be attentive to the attitudes you are observing. Does your recovering friend act as if all hope is gone, communicating to you that there is no light at the end of the tunnel? If you are sensing that this is the case, you may want to help them to seek the advice of a psychiatrist. Clinical depression is best diagnosed and treated by a professional.

Medication for Depression

Sometimes a doctor will recommend medication for depression, but recovering users may reject this option with a stubbornness that is detrimental to their well-being. In other words, an addict may refuse to consider medication that could bring great benefit. Understandably, they conclude with conviction, *I just got off drugs—the last thing I want to do is start taking something else.*

But we should keep in mind that not all medications are bad. People with asthma, allergies, diabetes, or heart problems routinely take medication to treat their symptoms. Lives are vastly improved when people take *proper* medications. But it is also important for recovering individuals to make their own wise choices, weighing all the options with the help of family, physicians, and friends.

We should keep in mind that not all medications are bad.

Medications that relieve depression are called SSRIs (selective serotonin reuptake inhibitors). For many people, drugs in this category are making a huge difference. After thirty years in recovery, I have found this to be true for myself. My treatment for hepatitis C and years of substance abuse left me with low serotonin levels, and such prescriptions have really helped.

I grappled long and hard with this decision. I sought a second and third professional opinion, and all three doctors gave me the same medical advice, so I knew I could move forward with confidence. My suggestion to you would be to make sure you receive sound advice from your family doctor, and you may need to seek advice beyond that. Over the years, I've become a kind of health nut. I'm very careful about my health, and I also talk over issues like this with my wife. After discussing the pros and cons as a couple, we agreed that medication was the right decision for me.

Chapter 30
Relapse: Plan on It

What to do if your loved one relapses?

Is Relapse Part of Recovery?

Addiction has been called a *chronic relapsing disease.* Relapse is when the person in recovery chooses to try some controlled using again after attempting to remain abstinent. We know that addicts/alcoholics can't control substance use. If they could, they wouldn't be in this situation in the first place. Relapse is one more failed attempt at trying to control how much they are able to use.

Using a substance occasionally and in moderation isn't a problem for social drinkers. But once someone crosses over to habitual and uncontrolled use, there is no going back. Attempts to regain control—to use alcohol or drugs socially and occasionally—are common, and these attempts lead to relapses. Statistics show that approximately 90 percent of those who complete treatment will have a relapse—sometimes referred to as a *slip.*

Five months after leaving treatment in April, I tried just one more time to see if I could control my using. I went out with an old friend and drank.

I don't remember if I called Gary or he called me. Gary and I used to take drugs together. He was a good friend. We had known each other since high school. He knew I had quit, but he didn't know much about recovery. We hadn't seen each other for months, since before I had gone to the treatment center. We went out to a bar. I don't think I had any intention of drinking. After an hour or two of playing pool and being in the midst of a crowd of people who were drinking, I ordered a beer. To this day, I don't know what I was thinking. After five or six beers, I knew I had screwed up. I wasn't nearly as wasted as I wanted to be. What now? Because of everything I had heard in recovery groups, I now felt a

> *Relapse is one more failed attempt at trying to control how much he is able to use.*

tremendous sense of guilt. Why did I let this happen? Looking back on it, I can see that it was a chain of events. Talking with Gary, meeting him at a bar, staying and playing pool—all the sights, sounds and smells were too much for me in the beginning of my sobriety. A bad idea. Those few drinks did not give me the effect I craved. I realized that it was going to take much more than a few drinks. I didn't want that old life back and it became obvious to me that I had to make an *all or nothing* choice.

It was just one night, but that one night motivated me to get right back to working on my recovery. This would fall into the category of a *slip*—one stupid decision that was brief and over quickly. I guess I just had to test the water one more time. What this experience did was confirm to me that my addiction was *real*. I felt like an idiot. I had just blown one hundred fifty days of sobriety, and I didn't even enjoy it.

Having a few drinks had always been the start of trouble for me. I knew I had to come to my senses right away, or I would soon be looking for drugs as well. This *small slip* would end up as a complete return to full-blown using, or I could end it that night. By this time in my recovery, I had learned enough to know what was happening and what the consequences could be. I must have had a moment of clarity. Nobody needed to tell me that I'd screwed up. Going back to the old life was the last thing I wanted.

I wasn't sure what to do, so I decided to go back to my treatment center for a couple of days to sort this out.

> "A few months after leaving Valley Hope, Joe went out drinking with an old friend. He called and asked us to drive him back to Valley Hope. While he was there, he got back on track over the weekend and came home again."
>
> —*Gladys Herzanek*

I have heard similar stories from others who have relapsed. Many of them remember that exact, pivotal moment when they were faced with the decision of what to do. Here are the two different trains of thought that can occur to an addict after a relapse. *I've blown it anyway, so I may as well keep using for a while.* Or, *This was a dumb idea. I'd better get right back to recovery before it gets much worse.* Thankfully, the latter was my thinking.

Ways to Avoid Relapse

Developing relationships with others who are facing the same challenges are very important. A couple of close friends, a sponsor, a mentor—any one of these—can help hold a person accountable. I knew I had let some people down. But these same people were able to encourage me to keep moving forward.

One of the results of an addict spending time with people in recovery is that it will ruin their once seemingly gratifying relationship with alcohol and drug use. Those in recovery learn about the disease, and from that point on they know too much about its power to ever enjoy it the way they used to. They know that there's no going back. If someone *slips,* they often feel the way I did—like an idiot for even trying to enjoy it again. But this is all okay, as we all learn from mistakes like this. Family and friends shouldn't get too discouraged when someone slips, because it's common in early recovery. Look at it as one more opportunity for your loved one to become convinced that the addiction is indeed real.

My friend and addiction counselor Larry Weckbaugh in Eagle, CO compares recovery to a series of stairs—and landings in-between the flights. The addict might be up three flights and two landings when they relapse. They don't fall into the basement; they only go down one floor.

> *Success seems to be connected to action.*
> *Successful people keep moving.*
> *They make mistakes but they don't quit.*
>
> *—Conrad Hilton*

Is there a difference between a slip and a relapse?

Sort of. The difference lies in how a person handles it. A slip is when someone goes back out to drink or use drugs, screws up, realizes it, and gets right back to working on their recovery. A full-blown relapse would be when a person goes back to using and *stays gone* for a period of time, which is tragically long enough to get right back to the bottom of the pit they climbed out of.

I am in no way suggesting that anyone should slip or relapse to test his addiction for even one night. One night can easily turn into one thousand nights; some may never return. What I am saying is that a person who has slipped shouldn't beat himself up over it. And families need to help the addict move forward and keep trying. As a concerned loved one, you may experience heart-wrenching disappointment when you see a user fall. But remember, all hope is not lost. The addict should just return to attending groups or meetings, learn the lesson, and move on.

> *... one thing I do: Forgetting what is behind*
> *and straining toward what is ahead,*
> *I press on toward the goal to win the prize*
> *for which God has called me ...*
>
> *—Philippians 3:13-14*

Why does relapse happen and what are the triggers?

The number one reason for a slip or relapse is stress, stress that is building to a seemingly uncontrollable level. Webster's Dictionary defines stress as *physical, mental, or emotional tension or strain*. A little stress is a normal part of life and can even be good for us. The problem, of course, occurs when stress builds to an unmanageable level.

People learn to cope with stress in different ways. What works best for me is exercise and communication. Talking things through with other users, and with my family, makes all the difference. Exercise helps to eliminate the effects of stress on my body and talking works the same way for my mind. As a person in recovery, I know how I used to handle the stress of life—with some form of medication. This method never solved anything.

I've heard it said that the only people who never experience stress are in cemeteries. Connecting with others who have had similar stressors is one good way to lighten your burdens. To know you are not alone, that you're not the only one struggling, is comforting. This is especially true for a person in recovery. But the *cause* of a person's stress is not the issue. Life will always have its problems. Rather, how someone chooses to deal with the challenges of life is what matters. Family and friends need to know that not properly handling these inevitable frustrations is the number one cause for relapse.

Understanding Relapse

Even after reading this chapter, you may still have trouble understanding why a relapse may happen. I'm a recovering addict, it happened to me, and it's hard for me to completely understand as well. The truth is that a recovering addict may relapse several times. The best thing to do is to try to remain hopeful, and encourage the person to keep on fighting the battle, though you may feel anger, frustration, and disappointment. Getting some support from others in the family, and from groups such as Al-Anon, will be helpful. And try to remember that the recovering person will feel these feelings as intensely as you do.

I would recommend going to some "open" AA meetings. This is a superb resource for families. Open meetings are for anyone interested in this topic. Just sit and listen as others share what it was like for them and how they got sober.

Relapse is similar to a cancer that comes out of remission. It doesn't do any good to get mad at the cancer or the person. The same is true for the disease of addiction. Instead, try to focus on the solution, which is to get your loved one sober and drug-free. Eventually, with the help of family and the right support, those in recovery will stop relapsing, regardless if they've had one relapse or a dozen.

Relapse Happens

Some who are reading this may have already observed several relapses. You may be asking, *When will it ever stop?* You can take comfort in knowing that a majority of people in recovery will have a few relapses. For a small minority, it could be much worse, and additional long-term treatment may be necessary.

A very good friend of mine works in the recovery field. Nick has abstained from drugs and alcohol for almost twenty years. His life is good, his marriage is solid, and he has a teenage son who is doing great.

But years ago, I don't know of anyone who appeared to be more hopeless. I can only imagine what it must have been like for his family, going through relapse after relapse after relapse. Nick went through eight different treatment centers before he finally *got it.*

The day of his last relapse was very stressful for him. He was living in a halfway house at the time. Halfway houses usually have many rules and everyone is assigned different chores, such as cooking and cleaning. After lunch Nick skipped his cleanup assignment, walked two blocks, and bought a half-pint of vodka. Before the bottle was gone, he was on the phone buying crack. This crack binge lasted a few days and he soon had another warrant out for his arrest. He was offered the choice of going through another treatment program or returning to prison. That was twenty years ago.

> *Patience, persistence and perspiration*
> *make an unbeatable combination for success.*
> —*Napoleon Hill*

Since then, he has helped hundreds of other men, women, and their families battle this same addiction. Nick is now highly respected in his field, loves his work, and will continue to be an inspiration for countless others in the future. He is just one more example to me of how anyone can overcome addiction.

A Bad Combination

The combination of stress and "triggers" can be a real problem. We have all heard about Dr. Pavlov and his experiment with dogs. He fed his dogs and at the same time rang a bell. He did this over and over, and eventually the dogs would salivate every time he rang the bell—whether there was food around or not. Looking back on my own drug use, I remember experiencing similar feelings of anticipation. Knowing my drug dealer was coming over, seeing a mirror with a razor blade on it, smelling the drug—all these things excited my brain. With no real conscious effort, I would start to mentally drool, knowing what was coming next. I learned, just like Dr. Pavlov, that once this subconscious change has taken place, a person can't just turn it off. *There is no on/off switch.* These things become imprinted on the brain. Over time they will fade and eventually go away.

This is true for many things in life. A particular song, smell, or place can trigger memories that a person hasn't thought of for years. The brain is very powerful, and potentially life-threatening triggers should not be taken lightly. Socializing with people who drink and use drugs can be a trigger. Going to a bar, with all its familiar sights, sounds, and smells, can be a trigger. Mirrors, razor blades, rolling papers, certain music—any or all of these things—can trigger a relapse.

People often ask about the dangers of ingesting seemingly harmless food and drink, such as cough syrup, food cooked with wine or liqueurs or drinking a small amount of wine during communion. Should a recovering person stay away from such things? Yes. Even these items can be invitations for relapse.

> *To go against the dominant thinking*
> *of your friends,*
> *of most of the people you see every day,*
> *is perhaps the most difficult*
> *act of heroism you can perform.*
> —*Theodore White*

When I quit using, I had to go through my apartment and get rid of all kinds of things that could be triggers to me. I looked for anything that had to do with my drug use: rolling papers, pipes, small vials for coke, pictures of drugs, baggies with any residue in them, scales—you name it. I also knew that I couldn't hang around with any of my old friends who were mostly drug dealers or heavy drug users. That wasn't easy. Though they were not good for me, I still felt a camaraderie with some of them. A few didn't believe the change in me would last. Several times they tried to get together with me to party. I had to say "no" and explain why. This time of letting go was difficult and awkward, but I found it wasn't impossible to leave these relationships behind. After a while, I began to see that many of these friendships were pretty lame anyway.

> *Being in recovery*
> *and hanging out with old friends*
> *wasn't going to work.*
> *It would be like going to a crack house*
> *and asking for a seat in non-smoking.*
>
> —*Barry W.*

In the case of a recovering teen, saying *no* to these things needs to come from deep within—not from a command from Mom, Dad or spouse. When parents try pulling their children away from other troubled peers, it is never as effective as when teenagers make the decision themselves. In fact, the parental control can often have the reverse effect—with the teen adamantly resolving, *You can't tell me who my friends can be!*

I had to learn new ways to handle both stress and triggers. For me, triggers (people, places, and things) were easier to cope with than stress.

Triggers were avoidable, whereas stress wasn't. Today, I continue to work on and improve my response to daily stress. Time and experience are wonderful teachers, which over the years have helped to mellow my response to everyday stress.

> "We couldn't visit him during the first week. The second week we went to see him, and he was really doing good. He had a smile and that was so great to see. The third week he came home for the weekend. He called one evening during that weekend while I was at work and said, 'Mom there is a half bottle of Vodka here, and I wondered if I could pour it down the sink.' I said of course!"
>
> —*Gladys Herzanek*

Once a person has had several years in recovery, all these issues lessen in intensity. I'm thankful that today my relationships with people are much healthier. I don't have any friends who abuse alcohol or use drugs. I no longer have anything in common with users. They are as uncomfortable around me as I am around them.

Looking back to when alcohol and drugs controlled me, I can see that my old way of living bred a level of stress that stemmed mainly from heavy using. Although I have been sober now for over thirty years, stressful times are still part of my life, but now I am able to handle them in healthy ways. What has changed is my attitude.

> *So let's not get tired of doing what is good.*
> *At just the right time we will reap*
> *a harvest of blessing if we don't give up.*
>
> —*Galatians 6:9 (NLT)*

DON'T QUIT

When things go wrong, as they sometimes will,
When the road you're trudging seems all uphill,
When the funds are low and the debts are high,
And you want to smile, but you have to sigh,
When care is pressing you down a bit,
Rest, if you must, but don't you quit.

Life is queer with its twists and turns,
As every one of us sometimes learns,
And many a failure turns about,
He might have won had he stuck it out;
Don't give up though the pace seems slow—
You may succeed with another blow.

Success is failure turned inside out—
The silver tint of the clouds of doubt,
And you never can tell how close you are,
It may be near when it seems so far,
So stick to the fight when you're hardest hit—
It's when things seem worst that you must not quit.

—*Author unknown*

Chapter 31
They're BAAaaack!

What should you do when he comes back from treatment?

What Now?

When the recovering person comes home from treatment, the real journey is about to begin. They have just been immersed in a crash course—*Everything you need to know about addiction and how to live substance free.* Coming home is an important event. How successfully will your husband apply his newfound wisdom? Will your friend be able to make a lasting change now that she is back in the real world? Remember, they just left a safe place where they made friends and received daily encouragement—and now they are back, facing many of the harsh realities of life.

Most likely, your loved one will feel a real sense of accomplishment, having successfully completed the program. Having confidence that he can start a new life is a good thing. At the same time, however, he is about to receive his first dose of reality. Now all the knowledge he gained about recovery must be practically lived out. He is going to have a myriad of questions: *How do I tell old friends about my new life? How are they going to react? How am I going to react if they aren't supportive of my new lifestyle? Will I have the strength? What will I say? Who should I see and who should I avoid? What do I need to start doing right now to avoid using again? Where will I find a new group to belong to? What if I don't find a group of people I like? How hard do I have to work to stay away from alcohol or drugs? Do I have what it takes to do this?*

> *Inaction breeds doubt and fear.*
> *Action breeds confidence and courage.*
> *If you want to conquer fear,*
> *do not sit home and think about it.*
> *Go out and get busy.*
> —*Dale Carnegie*

Seek Support

All recovering addicts must decide what they need to do to continue their lives in recovery with success and then follow through with action—all by themselves. In light of their own circumstances, only they can take the next step. Obviously many people and groups can be helpful, but it's the individual that must decide to seek out the support that will make his commitment to change successful. This needs to happen soon. Some form of support will be needed to keep this recovery ball rolling, whether it's AA, NA, an outpatient group, or counseling. This period of time, when the person has just returned home, is when all the talk and good intentions need to turn into positive action.

It should not take long to determine the sincerity of the recovering person. Actions speak louder than words, and *no one* successfully recovers alone. How much and how long the person makes use of outside support will depend on the situation, but everyone will need some form of support as they adjust to life on life's terms.

> "Joe was in Valley Hope for five weeks. It was a miracle! He was great when he came home. I'm sure he was a bit unsure just how long he could go without drugs. He did great, and even got a *real* job."
> —*Gladys Herzanek*

What to Do

So as a family member or friend, what do you do? If possible, anticipate this situation by meeting with treatment staff for sound advice before your loved one comes home. This can be a time to debrief and get answers to some of your questions. Try not to be overly self-conscious about what you do or say to the person returning home. You don't need to be walking on eggshells. Talking about recovery and encouraging someone is a good thing. By the same token, recovery shouldn't dominate all discussions. The process is just beginning, and you should give it time. The recovering person is trying to build a new life—one they can call *normal.* The more they see that life can be normal without using, and that they can deal successfully with everyday situations, the more motivated and encouraged they will be to continue with sober living. It may take time, but it does become easier.

When I returned home after treatment, I was both confident and scared at the same time. I know that sounds like a contradiction, but it's true. I was having an internal battle: part of me believed that I would do whatever it took to stay away from drugs, but another part of me wasn't sure about the "do whatever it takes" strategy that we had discussed in treatment. My family knew it wasn't going to be easy. For the most part, they left me alone. When they saw that I made the effort to go to work and regularly attend my group meetings, the atmosphere gradually grew more relaxed. They saw that I was moving in the right direction and seemed to discern that it was okay to trust me. I'm glad they gave me some space. I guess they knew they didn't have the answers I needed anyway. Only another recovering person can really understand what it's like, so my parents and family could not fully put themselves in my situation. Their ability to understand what I was going through was limited, yet I needed their support. This is when I began to spend a lot of time with other recovering people.

Not everyone will be able to go to a residential treatment center; therefore, recovery will look a little different in such cases. It will mean attending a lot of evening and weekend groups. A healthy level of busyness can help ensure sobriety.

Only another recovering person can really understand what it's like.

Work and recovery should be the two main priorities for those in recovery. If your loved one is not working, then that means they should spend more time attending groups. Idle time can be a strong temptation to revert to old habits.

For families in this recovery situation, encouraging the recovering addict to continue with his new life and not give up will take a great deal of patience. Because the user has not been totally removed from his life setting, it may take longer for him to become strong. Remember, you have a limited understanding of addiction and recovery, so attending some Al-Anon or "open" AA meetings would be an excellent idea. This will give you more knowledge about what your loved one might be going through. In addition, these meetings are a way for people in similar situations to connect and give one another support and advice. Attending these meetings is also a *huge sign of support* from you to your friend or loved one.

In some cases, it would benefit the recovering person to temporarily relocate. If they can live with a relative or friend for a few months, it will give them a chance to concentrate on their recovery without the pressures of dealing with old buddies, bad influences, and triggers that can cause a relapse.

If you have been a positive influence in this person's life, continue that support. However, you

Be yourself. Help them to have fun without using. Be a friend.

will need to provide a healthy balance of support. Don't smother them with an unusual amount of concern, as this will make them feel self-conscious. On the other hand, don't distance yourself, because you may be afraid and unsure how to act around them. Be yourself. Help them to see that life without using can be fun. They may have been afraid of losing all their friends, including you. Be a friend. Good friends who don't use are what they need.

> ## *I'm going through a humbling experience . . .*
> *—Richard Pryor*

It won't take long to figure out how serious your loved one is about their new life. Their attitude will be one indication of how they are adjusting. Admitting complete defeat in the face of addiction is a humbling experience. In my case, life in recovery meant acting differently than I did before: striving to listen to others without overreacting, and learning how to be patient. This again is a process that takes time. Some moodiness should be expected, but if it persists it needs to be addressed, as it could be a sign of too much stress. It could also be a result of the void created by not using, sadness from losing old friends, and abandoning an old lifestyle that defined who they were.

There will be some peaks and valleys in early recovery. Remember: If relapse occurs, don't be too harsh. Rather, be concerned about the next step they need to take. If your struggling friend gets right back to their recovery program, then stay as optimistic as possible. And when they fall down, help them to get back up and moving in the right direction. Remember, recovery is a process, and your relationship with your friend or loved one can greatly impact their desire to stay on course and make the right choices.

Conclusion

So what is my vision for this book? If just a handful of lives are changed, it will have been worth it all. But my hopes are much higher than that. The problem of addiction is costing a lot more than dollars. Families are being devastated because of drugs and alcohol. My belief is that gaining knowledge helps a concerned person play an integral role in finding solutions. What you have just read in this book is my firsthand knowledge about addiction—what I believe can make a difference.

I know that recovery is possible for anyone who earnestly seeks it. You've probably heard the idea that when we come to the end of our lives, there will be only two things that were important: who we loved, and who loved us. Recovery from addictions enables us to love others in a healthy way, allowing us to leave a legacy of healthy relationships. Recovery opens doors that have been closed, sometimes for years.

Love is a noun, but it is also a verb. To love is to make a commitment. It's easy to love when all is well. But what about when times are tough? When a couple gets married, they promise to love each other *for better or for worse*. Love is tough; it's not always easy to do the right thing. At times, love means allowing someone to suffer and feel pain. From some of the examples in this book, you can see that pain can be a great teacher when dealing with addiction. In my own steps toward recovery, it taught me a lot. I needed to be humbled; I needed to be willing to ask for help. Pain enabled me to be open to receive the help I needed. I'm grateful that my family loved me enough to allow me to suffer. I know it wasn't easy for them. My mother recalls the time when she intervened as the hardest thing she and my dad ever had to do.

My son, Jake, once quoted Nietzsche's statement about hard times: "What doesn't kill us

I'm grateful that my family loved me enough to allow me to suffer.

only makes us stronger." Regardless of the amount of unfairness that enters our life, we can still overcome and move on. I once thought my set of circumstances justified my behavior. When people criticized me I thought, *If you only knew my problems, you would understand.* Over the past few decades, I have heard story after story from addicts about how unfair life can be. But regardless of the amount of unfairness we have experienced, we must make peace with it—or allow it to destroy us. The choice is ours.

> *If people have a basic understanding*
> *of right from wrong,*
> *possess a strong desire to better themselves*
> *and persist in their cause,*
> *they can break the chain*
> *of any negative environment.*
>
> —*Dave Pelzer*

In the early '70s, a boy named David Pelzer was removed from his home by California's Child Services Department. He was considered one of the three worst victims of child abuse in California's history. From the age of five to nine, he had been abused by his alcoholic mother. David survived profound brutality at the hand of someone who was supposed to have loved him. He was routinely starved, forced to live in the basement and sleep on the floor, made to drink a combination of cleaning chemicals, forced to eat feces, burned over an open flame, and suffered broken bones inflicted by his mother. By the time Child Services stepped in, his mother had changed his name to "It."

David grew up in foster homes, managed to complete high school and college, and later joined the Air Force to fulfill his dream of flying jets. He has authored books depicting the human potential to overcome adversity, including his autobiography, *A Child Called "It,"* and is a motivational speaker with a great sense of humor. Life was not fair to David Pelzer. But David chose to use his past to inspire others to find the strength, hope, and courage to build a new life.

There are other *David Pelzers* in the world. If anyone ever had a legitimate excuse to kill his memories, this man did. Yet he refused to let them be the end of his story.

Your loved one hasn't reached the end of his story either. People who want to make positive changes badly enough can make radical changes in their lives. Don't give up. Fight the good fight, both for the sake of your loved one, and for yourself.

> *He lifted me out of the slimy pit,*
> *out of the mud and mire;*
> *he set my feet on a rock*
> *and gave me a firm place to stand.*
>
> —*Psalm 40:2*

We've touched on a lot of different aspects of addiction and the family dynamic, and you may feel as if you are just beginning to grasp an understanding of addiction and its complexities. My hope is that you have found answers that will help you to endure the hard times, equipping you with enough information to approach professionals and counselors in your community. The question, *Why Don't They Just Quit?*, will continue to be asked often in our quick-fix society. And now, perhaps you can help your friends and family begin to answer this question.

I trust you found glimpses of hope throughout this book that can help you support your loved one. I believe that your family and relationships can be fully restored and that you can help break the cycle of addiction. Starting today, you can begin to build a brighter future for those you love. I believe you will.

Part 4 Overview:
Key Points to Remember

- Recovery is a rewarding, exciting journey.

- Healing the mind requires outside help.

- There is no secret "miracle pill" to heal the body.

- Vigorous exercise produces feel-good chemicals in the brain and relieves stress.

- Spiritual fulfillment is equal in importance to healing the mind and body.

- Some medications used during withdrawal may help ease symptoms.

- Use of medications by a recovering person needs to be monitored by a physician.

- Always dispose of unused medications—especially pain meds.

- Some people in recovery experience clinical depression. Do not be afraid to seek help.

- Relapse is not uncommon. If it occurs, use it as a learning experience and move on.

- There is a difference between a slip and a relapse.

- Understand and avoid triggers.

- Never forget Step One.

- Support a newly recovering person, but do not try to closely monitor them.

- A temporary change in environment may be helpful in early recovery.

- There is no quick fix; people don't *just quit.*

- Recovery is within reach for anyone, and it really is a fulfilling, victorious lifestyle.

Part 5

Q&A with Joe

HOW CAN I TELL?

Q *How can I tell if someone is an addict/alcoholic or just a heavy user?*

A. *It is almost impossible to tell when someone has crossed this line.*

What you will be able to see, however, are the signs of dependency. Sometimes these signs will be subtle and other times they'll be more obvious. Here are a few questions regarding behavioral signs that may signal dependency:

- Has this person's attitude changed?
- Are they using daily?
- Are they unable to control how much they are using?
- Are they defensive about their using?
- Has work or school performance declined?
- How long has this persisted? Do they try to hide their use?
- Have they lost interest in people or activities that were once important to them?

Beyond these, there may be more obvious signs such as legal problems, DUIs, or frequent job changes. Seeking advice from a professional is always a good idea. You may also take a self-test. It you're concerned about this person, you probably know him or her fairly well. Take the self-test for alcoholism/drug addiction found in Appendix B of this book and answer as if you were your friend or loved one. See how well *you* score.

Develop a built-in "B.S. detector."
—*Ernest Hemingway*

Q How can I know if my addicted friend or loved one is telling me the truth?

A.   *Most of the time, you can't.*

There is no hard and fast test for honesty in a person—especially a substance abuser. Don't be surprised or terribly hurt if and when a recovering person fails to tell you the truth. I have done this myself, and seen it during my interactions with the men and women I've counseled over the years (particularly those in the jails and prisons). The thought life of the chemically dependent person is all about the drug—24/7/365.

When I was using drugs, I planned my days around getting high. When someone asked me what I'd been doing, where I was going, where I'd been, why I needed money, or when I would be back, I just made things up. Honesty would only have caused more problems for me. My attitude was, *I'll tell you whatever I need to say to get you off my back.*

This is one reason recovery is difficult at first, since it means being honest for the first time in a long time.

Q *Are passing out and blacking out the same thing?*

A.   No.

Both of these terms are often associated with alcohol use. Elsewhere in this book, we speak of alcohol as being a sedative/hypnotic drug. Passing out from drinking too much alcohol is definitely a sign of being sedated and/or drunk. **Passing out** is what is referred to when a person becomes unconscious, similar to going to sleep.

Blacking out is completely different from passing out. In fact, the word *hypnotic* (as in sedative/hypnotic) is one way to think about blackouts. For instance, someone who has been hypnotized can appear to function normally; they can follow commands, and so on. When the hypnotic state is over, they often can't remember what they have done.

A blackout is like a temporary form of amnesia. Alcohol can and does affect our memory. Short-term memory loss is what happens after a person has experienced a blackout. The user may not have to be very drunk for this to happen. They will appear to be functioning normally—carrying on a conversation, driving a car, playing a game, watching a movie, or even having sex—yet not remember the events the following day. This condition will also worsen over time; blackouts will start happening more often and the person will remember less. Blackouts happen to many, but not all drinkers. Others may reach a point where it happens every time they drink—even after the first drink of the evening. Some drugs can create this experience as well.

Q *If someone can stop using for weeks at a time, they "aren't" an addict—correct?*

A. *Not necessarily.*

I've seen a few instances where an addict/alcoholic will stop using for weeks at a time. They might stop because of a bad consequence that occurred, or maybe their spouse moved out, or they've encountered a legal problem of some kind. There are even some people who develop a pattern of this; they abstain for a period and then go on a binge. The real issue is still one of control. When using, can they control their use? For the alcoholic/addict, the answer is always the same: *No.*

DOES IT HAVE TO BE?

> *There were a couple of things in the intervention*
> *that made me know I needed help.*
> *One was a letter from my daughter saying*
> *that she was ashamed*
> *she had the same last name as I did . . .*
> —*Pat Summerall*

Q *Does an intervention have to be a surprise attack?*

A.   No.

Most people think of an intervention as a type of ambush, but it doesn't have to happen like that. Just one person can conduct an intervention, and it can be as casual and relaxed as a conversation over coffee. Also, if the intervention is carried out by a professional, a few phone calls to the addict or alcoholic could be all it takes.

How an intervention is approached will depend on the situation and the person with the problem. For some, the surprise type of intervention may be the best approach. I would advise people to talk it through with a treatment center or professional, and then make the choice that seems best. It's important to plan when to approach your loved one, and then what to say. An ideal time is shortly after they have been on a binge, or when they have a hangover.

Q *If both parents are addicts, does that increase the child's chances of addiction?*

A.   *There is a fifty-fifty chance.*

The more alcoholics there are in a family, the higher the odds of passing along this addiction. In fact, when both parents have had substance abuse issues, the odds are 50/50 that their children will as well—should they decide to experiment with alcohol or drugs.

So what does that mean? In a case where both parents have a problem, with the odds at 50/50, will half of the kids become addicts? Not necessarily. This is an *average*. But it does mean the likelihood of becoming dependent is very high. Knowing this can help families recognize warning signs earlier rather than later. Depending on their maturity level, children and teenagers may decide to wait until early adulthood to begin experimentation. (Or as in the case with our daughter, they may decide not to start at all.)

Parents and other family members with such histories can consider how to help their children avoid developing a substance abuse problem. It is also a good idea for them to educate their children as to what is likely to happen if they are not on their guard. Knowing the dangers, facts, and warning signs of addiction is helpful, especially for those with a genetic predisposition. If we can get these kids to even *delay* trying drugs or alcohol, it will help to lessen their chances of falling into a life of dependency. Many research studies show that the later someone waits to start using, the less likely they are to become dependent.

WHAT IS IT?

Q *What does the term "pink cloud" mean?*

A. *It means to feel almost like being high, but without using drugs or alcohol.*

The first few days or weeks in recovery are normally a time of adjustment for the addict's body and mind. Early recovery can be a rollercoaster of emotions—often frustrating and stressful.

After this will come a leveling-out period in which many people will have an almost euphoric feeling, sometimes referred to as a "pink cloud." This *ah-ha* experience can last for days or even weeks—*I really have this recovery thing figured out; I can do this!* I remember feeling this way myself. It was almost like a natural high. But the addict should be careful not to think that he or she is cured, because this could lead to another try at controlled using (i.e., a slip or relapse). Five months after leaving treatment I tried some *controlled using.* For me this verified that I indeed was addicted, and I quickly got back to working on my recovery. A person in recovery can almost plan on experiencing a pink cloud, but the ensuing relapse doesn't have to happen.

> *I fell off my pink cloud with a thud.*
>
> —*Elizabeth Taylor*

Q *Isn't addiction just a willpower problem?*

A.   No.

When men or women *begin* using alcohol or drugs, willpower does play an important role. Deciding to drink or use drugs the first few times is simply a choice. The person may find the initial experiences enjoyable and pleasurable, but that doesn't make them an addict or alcoholic. Certain drugs can have a much more powerful effect than others, which the user may want to repeat. Just the same, it takes time to become physically and mentally dependent.

> *We may think there is willpower involved,*
> *but more likely . . . change is due to "want power"*
> *. . . wanting the new me*
> *in preference to the person I am now.*
>
> —*George A. Sheehan*

Over time, the brain and central nervous system will expect the drug to come in from the outside. This is where physical dependence begins: stopping the use now will result in some signs of withdrawal. Mental or psychological dependence also plays a role in addiction. Once the person develops a physical and mental dependency (i.e. an obsession), willpower becomes less effective. The longer a person continues to use and build tolerance, the more difficult it is to *just quit* with willpower alone.

There is much to be said regarding this subject of willpower, or lack of it. Many recovering people swear, *If not for a power greater than myself, I would still be using.* Many addicts who recognize their need to quit do not *want* to quit. Where then will this desire come from?

Whether this power comes from the person's spiritual life, or the power of their group or caring friends, recovering people recognize that sheer willpower does not work for them. At some point in recovery, a desire to stop using manifests itself in a person's consciousness. Call it what you will; I call this a miracle.

Footprints in the Sand

One night I dreamed I was walking along the beach with the Lord. Many scenes from my life flashed across the sky.

In each scene I noticed footprints in the sand. Sometimes there were two sets of footprints, other times there was one only.

This bothered me because I noticed that during the low periods of my life, when I was suffering from anguish, sorrow or defeat, I could see only one set of footprints, so I said to the Lord,

"You promised me Lord, that if I followed you, you would walk with me always. But I have noticed that during the most trying periods of my life there has only been one set of footprints in the sand. Why, when I needed you most, have you not been there for me?"

The Lord replied, "The years when you have seen only one set of footprints, my child, is when I carried you."

—Author (still) unknown

Q *Does relapse mean failure?*

A.   No.

Since addiction/alcoholism is a chronic relapsing disease, relapse does not mean failure. For many men and women, recovery can be a pattern of two steps forward, one step back. Relapse, in a way, just confirms that the person does indeed have a problem. As crazy as this may sound, I would say to almost anyone: *Consider that it might happen, and then plan what to do if or when it does. After a relapse, the person should call a friend who is also in recovery and get right back to doing what is needed to avoid it in the future. Learn from it.* The recovering person should ask, *Why did this happen?* He needs to be honest. What triggered the event? Was it planned out? What events may have led up to it? Then be honest about what to do in order to ensure that it doesn't happen again.

> ### *You may have to fight a battle more than once to win it.*
> *—Margaret Thatcher*

Q *What is methadone? What is harm reduction?*

A.   Methadone hydrochloride is a synthetic opiate used as a form of "harm reduction" for heroin addicts. Harm reduction is intended as a progressive alternative to certain lifestyle choices such as casual sex, prostitution, and drug use.

The philosophy of harm reduction has developed over the years and the thinking goes like this: *Some people just won't quit no matter what; therefore, let's see what can be done so they do less harm to themselves and society.*

> *I used to inject methadone, but I lost fifty pounds.*
> *My limbs became just strings of muscle.*
> *When I could no longer find a place to inject,*
> *that was the end.*
>
> —*Bela Lugosi*

One initiative of harm reduction is a free government-sponsored program where methadone is given to heroin addicts in place of heroin. The high from the drug is very similar to the high from heroin, but it does not provide the euphoric rush and the high also lasts longer. It's given to heroin addicts so they won't have to commit crimes to get more money for dope. Methadone is given once a day and is taken orally in liquid or pill form. (Whether the person truly is a heroin addict and not just someone looking for free drugs can be determined by their arrest record, any previous unsuccessful treatment for heroin, or marks on the arms showing IV drug use.) Most people who begin the methadone maintenance program will be on it for life. The good news is that once a person becomes stable on methadone, they can function *normally*. They can work, drive a car, feel pain, and experience emotional reactions. Methadone relieves the craving associated with opiate addiction. The bad news is that methadone is more addictive than heroin, and the withdrawal symptoms are much more severe. Personal accounts from those who have experienced withdrawal from both heroin and methadone describe the withdrawal from methadone as *a living hell.*

My feeling is that taking methadone is like trading one drug for another. I am not a big fan of harm reduction. In my opinion, even heroin addicts can quit.

An additional drug that has become popular for withdrawal from opiates is Suboxone. This drug was originally intended to be used briefly for detox. Unfortunately, many will stay on this drug for a long time. Again, this appears to be another opportunity to switch from one drug to another.

Q *What is meant by a co-occurring disorder?*

A. *It's a psychological disorder that complicates treatment for drug addiction.*

It is estimated that in addition to their drug addiction, 10 to 20 percent of addicts/alcoholics have a separate psychological problem. In fact, many in this group view their alcohol or drug use as a form of self-medication. Depression, anxiety disorder, and bi-polar disease are just a few of the disorders that can further complicate treatment for addiction. Substance abuse will only make their other problem worse. If a co-occurring disorder is suspected, receiving professional advice is even more important. Still, recovery for these individuals is attainable. Proper diagnosis is the first step, because substance abuse can sometimes be the source of the addict's psychological problems.

A friend of mine from Miami, who is in his forties, just celebrated seventeen years of sobriety. I attended his celebration along with about fifty of his friends, relatives and colleagues. Early in life, before alcohol and drugs became a problem, he was already struggling—diagnosed as bi-polar and hospitalized twice for attempted suicide. He began to use alcohol and drugs to self-medicate. He told me that throughout his life he has been on thirteen different medications for depression and bi-polar disorder. He continues to take medication for bi-polar disorder, but has been alcohol- and drug-free since his early thirties. This is an example of someone who was fortunate to receive a proper diagnosis and who followed through on his recovery. The prescribed medications he takes now allow him to enjoy a much higher quality of life. For some people these medications are life-savers.

IS IT OKAY?

Q *Is it okay for a recovering addict to smoke pot?*

A.   No.

This has also been referred to as the "marijuana maintenance plan." Regardless of what a person's past drugs of choice were, smoking pot during recovery is a very bad idea. Many people who have tried this have ended up with one of two results: the same lack of control and abuse problem with smoking pot, or a return to their drug of choice.

Drug users tend to make poor choices while under the influence of any mind-altering drug. Good intentions fly out the window when any use begins. This is actually just an attempt to continue using something—anything—rather than remain substance free.

In order to set the record straight and make this simple, below are questions I am asked *over and over,* and I've included the answers I give *over and over.* Our persistent attempts to find a loophole can be quite humorous at times!

Q *Is it okay to smoke some weed once in a while?*

A: No.

Q *If I was a heroin addict and I quit that drug completely, is it okay to just smoke some weed?*

A: *No.*

Q *If I'm a recovering alcoholic, is it okay to smoke some weed?*

A: *No.*

Q *I'm in recovery, but since weed is found to grow naturally in many places, is it okay to just smoke weed?*

A: *No.*

Q *Since weed is not really a drug, is it okay to smoke some weed?*

A: *No.*

Q *I heard about a guy in recovery that smokes weed. Do you think I might be able to?*

A: *No.*

Q *There is an organization called NORMAL. If a group like this is able to get marijuana legalized, do you think I could just smoke weed?*

A: *No.*

Q *I've heard about smoking "medical marijuana" for people with health problems. What's up with this?*

A: *This is one really bad idea.*

> ### *What is the world coming to?*
> —*Ozzy Osborne*

Supposedly for pain relief, it is now possible to get a medical marijuana (MM) card. The typical MM card-holder is a twenty-three-year-old male. Even if it were true that we have high numbers of young males with chronic pain—smoking marijuana for "medical reasons" is still a mistake. First of all, it is very easy to just extract the active ingredient, THC, and use it in pill-form.

Why inhale the smoke into the lungs, other than to get the quicker rush, or "high" the drug produces? Secondly, this is one more way of throwing our hands up in the air and saying "People are just going to get stoned and there's nothing we can do about it." Do we, as a nation, want to make it easier for young people to get stoned? Personaly, I don't think so. Lastly, marijuana addiction is number three on the list of reasons people seek treatment. The first is alcohol, second is for opiates (pain meds) and then marijuana. After these three, come cocaine, and methamphetamine.

> "We owe it to the people we serve to speak out about the unintended consequences legalization (of marijuana) would have and the toll it would take on the health and safety of our communities."
>
> "Over the course of my career, from St. Petersburg to Seattle, I learned a lot about the damage drug abuse does to the fabric of our society—and about the terrible toll it takes on individuals, families and communities across this country," Kerlikowske told his former peers. "I'll never forget the rage and despair I felt when I worked undercover and I saw a drug dealer take a hit of marijuana—and then blow the smoke in the face of his toddler."
>
> —*Gil Kerlikowske, Director, Office of National Drug Control Policy (comments from a speech given at the International Conference of Chiefs of Police Annual Convention, October 23, 2009).*

Q *Is it okay for my teen to drink at home under my supervision?*

A.   No.

Some parents have come to believe that their teen is better off drinking or even smoking pot at home rather than out driving around with friends. This is a bad idea, and not just for legal issues. The message that it sends to an adolescent is, *I believe you have no self-control; you're going to use drugs no matter what, so use them at home where you'll be safe.* Adolescent brains are still *under construction* and substance use at an early age is not good for the brain. Even though your teen may experiment anyway, it is important to not condone such behavior. No matter what teens may say or even think, they do not need their parents to be their friends, nor should they expect parents to be their rescuers. They need strong parental guidance. Someone has to be the adult in the relationship.

> ### You can only be young once.
> ### But you can always be immature.
> —*Dave Barry*

Q Can I have alcohol in my home, or serve alcoholic drinks on social occasions?

A.   It depends how far into recovery the person is.

There are really two questions here. Let me take them one at a time. First, C*an I have alcohol in my home if I have a friend or loved one in recovery there as well?*

In the case of someone who is in early recovery, you should show some sensitivity. Having a few alternatives to alcoholic beverages, such as juice, sparkling water, and soft drinks, is helpful. If the user lives in your home or is staying for a period of time, then having alcoholic drinks around is not a good idea—especially if they are just beginning their recovery. If the person has successfully been in long-term recovery (by that I mean at least a few years), then this shouldn't be an issue.

The second question is: *Can I serve alcoholic drinks on social occasions if I know a recovering person will be attending?* If your social event includes a buffet or food choices, it's a very good idea to label food or punch bowls that have alcohol in them. There are other reasons people avoid alcohol—a person may be the designated driver, or taking medication that shouldn't be combined with alcohol, pregnant, or abiding by a strict diet. So letting people know the alcohol content of your food is a good practice in general and a common courtesy to extend.

Most recovering people understand that food cooked with wine, rum, or liqueurs will not be a problem, as the alcohol is cooked away. Some recovering people may not even want to consume food that has the *smell or flavor* of wine, as they know this can be a "trigger." People in long-term recovery, learn how to handle these situations. Just the same, let your guests know what has been cooked with alcohol. On the other hand, foods in which the alcohol is *not* cooked away, such as certain desserts, should be labeled as such. A little sensitivity in this area will be appreciated.

Q *Is it okay to tell your kids about your past use? How open should you be?*

A.   *Tell the truth, but there's no need to disclose everything.*

The thinking on this has changed over the years. We can't change the genes we pass on to our children, but we do have a choice about how much and what kind of information we pass on to them. How much do they *need to know?*

Even though honesty is the best policy, parents need to think from their child's point of view at times. As parents, we may have struggled for years with substance abuse, and done more than our fair share of using. Do our kids need to know that? We may think that being open with our children about our past proves that we can relate to the same peer pressure and experiences they are exposed to. Our motive is simply to warn them about the mistakes we made and hope they don't do the same. But what's the message they may be hearing? *Well, if Mom and Dad did it and they turned out okay in the long run, then why can't I?*

In the clinical field, experts are now advising that this amount of openness has the potential to backfire. How much do they really need to know? It may be a lot less than we realize. We should all think this through before sharing *everything*.

If parents do choose to share with their children *parts* of their past, they should be sensitive about what they say in order to educate and inform in a way that does not glorify addiction in *any* way. Those parents in recovery do have some valuable information to share, and if imparted wisely, their children will not only have a realistic understanding of the subject, but they may also be able to recognize warning signs. When they observe their classmates' poor choices and see a friend start to slip downhill, experience blackouts, or get in accidents, they will know what is happening because they will have been informed about it.

> *Be sure your brain is running,*
> *before you throw your mouth in gear.*
>
> —*Anonymous*

SHOULD I?

Q *Should I search my adolescent's room?*

A. **You bet.**

Not only should you search their room, but you should have no qualms about it. If you suspect he or she (a minor) might be using drugs or alcohol or be engaged in any other illegal activity, then you have an obligation to search. And by the way—aren't you paying the mortgage on the whole house?

Q *Should I be concerned about medications in my own bathroom?*

A. **Yes.**

Wanna get away? Most people have probably seen the airline commercial that I'm referring to. A person using the bathroom at a friend's house opens the medicine cabinet and a shelf falls and makes a lot of noise. The obvious implication is that the person gets caught snooping and wishes they could just "get away."

People in early recovery and those who *should be in recovery* may do some snooping when using your bathroom. Therefore, sleeping pills, leftover pain pills from a surgery, and any other medication should not be easily accessible. Before I entered my recovery, I would often check for these kinds of medications at a friend's house. For that matter, I'd check the medicine cabinets at the homes of anyone who would let me use the bathroom.

I have a friend who told me she would bring a meal over to a friend who may have had an accident or just returned from the hospital. Then she would politely ask to use the bathroom before leaving—with the hope of finding their prescription medications.

If you have adolescents at home, they may be checking as well. Even in the case where you are certain your own kids are not using, it still is a good idea to keep these out of sight. Your kids have friends who visit your home as well, and more and more adolescents are selling and using prescription drugs that they have obtained from others, including their friends' parents. A little caution with these medications may be prudent.

- Pharmaceuticals taken without a prescription or a doctor's supervision can be just as dangerous as taking illicit drugs or alcohol.
- Abusing painkillers is like abusing heroin because their ingredients (both are opiods) are very similar.
- Prescription medications are powerful substances. While sick people taking medication under a doctor's care can benefit enormously, prescription medication can have a very different impact on a well person.
- Many pills look pretty much the same, but depending on the drug and the dosage, the effects can vary greatly from mild to lethal.
- Prescription medications, as all drugs, can cause dangerous interactions with other drugs or chemicals in the body.

    —The Partnership for a Drug-Free America

Q *Should I be concerned when he talks about suicide?*

A.   Yes.

This is obviously something we cannot ignore. Threats of suicide, harming oneself or others are all serious concerns. So, what should we do?

First of all, you should talk with the person and make sure you are hearing him correctly. Secondly, you will have to decide how real or genuine the threat is. There is a big difference between someone saying "I hate my life" or saying "I plan to end it soon." Regardless of the tone of his comments, neither should be taken lightly.

You may want to get some immediate wise counsel to help with your next step. I would definitely talk with someone about your concern, and this should be a professional in the mental health field.

Having said all the above, let me talk about this in relation to the alcoholic/addict. It is quite common for the addict to get very depressed and not care much about living. This person is not enjoying life and sometimes will have thoughts of just wanting to "not be" anymore. As sad as this is, it is also extremely important to remember that it's rare for anyone to follow through on these thoughts. Some will even use this as a tactic to garner more sympathy and more support ($$) from family members.

In the rare circumstance that someone continues to talk about suicide or even follows through, you should keep a couple things in mind. Number one is that you can't keep him or her from taking this option. It is their poor choice and not your fault. Even though it is extremely rare, it does happen. Secondly, do seek help from other people and don't try to figure this out on your own. Lastly, don't let the addict use this threat like a big club to continually drain you of all your emotions and resources. There is help available to guide you through this issue.

I'M WONDERING . . .

Q *Does everyone have to know?*

A. No.

Most people may feel a little self-conscious about family, friends, and co-workers knowing of their problem. It's an issue that is hard to hide—especially if a person has gone away to treatment and returned. The recovering addict will often find that most of their friends and family members already knew that something had been wrong. Real friends are usually glad to see the changes. They may not understand addiction as a disease, but most will try to encourage the change. For the recovering person, I would say to feel free to discuss your recovery if the opportunity presents itself.

At the same time, there is what I call the "need to know factor." Some people just don't need to know all about our personal lives. I would recommend being selective about sharing this part of your life. In our society, there is still some stigma associated with alcohol and drug addictions.

I'll never forget a blind date I had early in my recovery. I was living in Miami and we went to a movie. In the car on the way there, I spoke about being in recovery. I didn't think much of it; I felt good about my new life, and it didn't bother me to be open about it. We arrived at the theatre, went in and sat down. A few minutes later she got up to go to the bathroom. After twenty minutes or so, I went to look for her. She was nowhere to be found. *Weird,* I thought. I finally decided to call her, and found out that she had felt uncomfortable and found a ride home. Way too much information for the short time we had known each other. I can laugh about it now, but I learned a good lesson.

Q *How can I show my love without enabling?*

A.   *Love is doing the right thing.*

Let's start with a definition for the word "enabling." Enabling is anything you do to help the addict to continue his or her substance use. The list of things could be quite long. Giving the person any financial help is often the biggest mistake, also—calling in for them when they can't get up for work of school, making excuses for them when they don't show up for important functions, like holidays, birthdays, weddings etc... Anything we do to help alleviate or lessen the consequences of their poor choices is enabling.

So how does one show love and concern without enabling? First of all I would let him or her know exactly what you intend to do. I would sit the person down and talk face-to-face (or write a letter) and say to them I love you and I want the best for you. My desire is to do whatever I can to help you in your journey to recover. At the same time, I will do nothing that enables you to continue a destructive lifestyle. As long as you choose this path, you are on your own. Let me know when you decide you want to start living life without drugs or alcohol.

> *A trap seizes him by the heel;*
> *a snare holds him fast.*
>
> —*Job 18:9*

Q *Is there a cure for addiction?*

A.   No.

Even quitting use completely does not mean someone is *cured*. Complete abstinence from alcohol or drugs is similar to a cancer in remission. As long as the addict/alcoholic does not start using again, his addiction will remain in remission. This is why the person will refer to himself as *recovering* instead of *recovered*.

One of the clear signs of addiction or alcoholism is lack of control. I have yet to meet the person who, once chemically dependent, has been able to return to responsible social use. If a person thought to be addicted successfully returns to social use, it means that he or she was not addicted in the first place. Sometimes people need to find this out for themselves before they are ready to seek help.

> *Hope changes everything, doesn't it?*
>
> —*Diane Sawyer*

Q *Are some people beyond hope for recovery?*

A.   *Almost Never.*

Other than a very small percentage of those who are severly mentally ill—I would say no. For every pathetic story of a life that appears beyond hope, there is also an equally dramatic story of recovery. What can happen is that some people may be beyond *help*. What I mean is that at some point the helper will need to step back and let the person experience their own epiphany, and too much helping can have the opposite effect. If *helping* turns to *continued rescuing,* the person never learns to solve his or her problems and becomes dependent on the *helper.* Getting an addiction professional involved for objective advice is important for tougher cases. It is important for the friend not only to get the advice, but to follow it as well. Never give up hope.

> *These things that are pleasin' you*
> *can hurt you somehow.*
>
> —The Eagles, *Desperado*

Q *Why is addiction called an "insidious" disease?*

A.   *Because it is.*

"Insidious" means to *spread harm in a subtle manner; to entrap in a seductive way.* Addicts or alcoholics may be the last ones to realize their dependence problem. The drug works in a seductive manner and its victim often doesn't realize what has happened until it's too late—a housewife realizes that she needs a glass of wine to keep her hands from trembling; a college student realizes that he drove home the previous night but can't remember doing so; a businessman finds that he needs to have multiple drinks throughout the day to maintain his façade. At this stage, the addict is often living in denial, trying to prove to himself and the world that he is in control.

No one likes to admit that they have been tricked. This is exactly what the drug is able to do. For the user, it is as though their best friend has betrayed them. Because of this slow and gradual process, most addicts aren't aware of what is happening to them and don't understand the changes taking place in their bodies and minds. When a user's brain ceases to function normally, he is no longer able to see clearly. People in recovery will often look back and say that it was as if their brain had been hijacked. This is why intervention is so important.

Q *What about babies born to addicted moms?*

A.   *They've got a fighting chance.*

Over the years we have heard about babies prenatally exposed to crack cocaine and methamphetamine. Many think that these infants will have multiple defects and problems as they develop. Although this can happen, it is not the norm by any means. Research has repeatedly shown that the environment in which these children grow up plays as big a role, if not bigger, in their development than does the drug to which they were exposed in utero. Many of these babies develop normally, and their prognosis for the future is also good. I have worked with a recovery center in Denver called The Haven that specializes in the treatment of addicted women who are new moms, most of whom are dependent upon methamphetamine. Over the past two years, over ninety percent of their babies have tested normal in physical and mental development.

The most damaging drug to an unborn child is alcohol. There is no safe alcohol limit for moms-to-be. For example, two women, each drinking the same quantity of alcohol, can produce different results: one baby born healthy, and another born with problems. Some women are not aware of the devastating consequences drinking can have on their unborn baby. Alcohol causes physical abnormalities to the brain and body. These abnormalities are Fetal Alcohol Syndrome Disorders (FASD), found in babies whose mothers drank alcohol during their pregnancies. FASDs are not curable, but they can be treated to minimize their impact on the children's lives and those of their families.

> ## It is much easier to suppress a first desire than to satisfy those that follow.
> —*Benjamin Franklin*

Q How does one respond to being offered a drink after beginning life in recovery?

A.   *Just say 'No thanks.'*

The first few times may be a little scary for the person as they wonder, *Will I have to explain why? What do I say? How do I say it? Is everyone going to know now?*

This was something my wife obsessed about when she was new in recovery. She remembers sitting at a big table of co-workers in a Mexican restaurant, and when the waitress came to their table, her friends ordered margaritas. She thought, *What am I going to say when it comes to me?* As it turned out, ordering a Diet Coke was not a big deal and no one really noticed. A polite "No thank you" is all that is necessary when the waiter offers the wine list. There are many reasons for not drinking other than addiction—medical reasons, dietary restrictions, being the designated driver, pregnancy, and just plain *not wanting to drink.* Saying *no* does not mean that you have to tell the world of your past.

For some people, this may be a bigger issue than for others. For this group, I would suggest developing a "canned response" and even practice it if necessary. Find a response that you are comfortable with—something like, "I'm done with that part of my life," or "I'm not doing that anymore."

Just being honest is also an option: "I found it was difficult to drink in moderation, so *I just quit,*" or "I've had enough to last me a lifetime." Who knows? This could actually inspire someone else to quit.

HOW CAN THEY?

Q *How can a mother or father leave their kids because of alcohol or drug use? Don't they love their kids?*

A.   *Yes, they do.*

This is one of the most baffling questions regarding addiction. Let's talk about fathers first, since I can speak from firsthand experience. Fathers who leave their children are perceived differently than women in the same situation. When I walked out on my wife and daughter, I felt bad about what I was doing. At the same time, my thinking was that my wife would now handle the child-rearing responsibilities. In my mind, I wasn't really *leaving* my daughter in the sense that I was leaving her all alone. I left because of my addiction. If you had asked me if I loved my daughter, I would have answered, "Of course I do." My actions, however, were sending a completely different message. Unfortunately, when a mother, because of her addiction, makes the same mistake, she is judged more harshly.

> "His actions affected me a lot. I felt rejected and unworthy. Jami [our daughter] was crushed—for years. I was afraid to be a single mom and was resentful that I had to be responsible. I began to drink more and party a lot. As a teen, Jami became very angry.

> He would be lost for weeks, undependable about showing up to see her, and when he did, he took her to fearful places. He wanted to be the big spender and live the rock star life. I was sad and truly believed he would return to us."
>
> —*Vicki, my former wife*

What we are observing in these instances is just how powerful substance addiction can become. At this point in addiction, it is nearly impossible to quit. The drug has complete control and users will do just about anything to get it. Even the maternal instinct women are born with may not be enough to motivate change. Mothers in this situation do love their children. At the same time, they may have become virtually powerless to stop the obsession that now consumes their entire being. This is often the point when a government agency may intervene. Children are the innocent victims and need to be in a safe place. This will often be the event that will motivate a parent to genuinely seek recovery.

IS IT TRUE?

Q *Are most addicts in jail, homeless, or unemployed?*

A.   No.

This is another misconception or myth. Only a small percentage of alcoholics and addicts fall into these categories. Most people with an alcohol or drug addiction do in fact have jobs, are not in jail, and are not homeless. There is a high likelihood that these events will happen eventually, but statistics show that about 77 percent of those with a substance abuse problem *do* have jobs.

It is only in later stages of addiction that men and women become unable to keep their jobs. Most alcoholics and addicts are not criminals. Their personal lives and their relationships with family and friends will suffer. Their physical health will also deteriorate. They may not be high-functioning employees on the job, but most will be able to maintain employment. This can go on for years—even decades.

Many addicts and alcoholics will even point to their gainful employment as *proof* that they don't have a problem. Only those closest to them may be able to recognize the problem and be able to help them do something about it.

> ## It's like deja-vu, all over again.
>
> —*Yogi Berra*

Q Does using drugs and alcohol change a person's brain chemistry?

A.   Yes.

Over time and with continued use, brain chemistry changes do occur when a person abuses drugs or alcohol. Our brains have a natural chemical balance. Certain chemicals in the brain, such as serotonin, help to stabilize our mood or feelings.

An addict's brain will begin to produce fewer of these chemicals on its own. Why? The brain shuts down production of these elements because it learns to expect them to come from an outside source—in the form of alcohol or drugs. As a user becomes more and more dependent, their brain chemistry is altered.

This is one more reason people experience mental discomfort during withdrawal from use. There is a lag time before the brain can start to produce these feel-good chemicals on its own. Over time, the brain will repair most if not all of the damage resulting from substance abuse, and the natural chemical balance will be restored.

Q Is it true that the chances for relapse are greater—the younger a person is?

A.   Yes.

It is generally true that younger people do have a more difficult time maintaining sobriety during early recovery. There are a couple of reasons for this. The first is that peer pressure is extremely powerful at this age. The desire to be accepted, be popular and have a "social life" is one most important elements in an adolescent's life. For teens and young adults, social gatherings very often include alcohol and some drug use. Secondly, they're just beginning to mature—and their coping skills to handle life's challenges haven't matured yet. These processes take years. Hence, it is true that the younger a person is, the more likely he is to relapse.

Q *Does heavy use of alcohol and drugs create addiction?*

A. *Sometimes.*

People who use alcohol and drugs in large quantities over time *may become addicted* to them. But this is not always the case. Only a percentage of users will become dependent. For many people, this period of heavy usage can be just a phase. Social and recreational alcohol and drug use lead some people to abusive use. During this period, there may be consequences, such as a DUI, and for many, these consequences will be enough to inspire them to quit or control their use. It is common to see college students, for example, drinking and using drugs while in school, but most will later become social drinkers capable of moderating their use.

For others, even multiple consequences will not have the same effect, and they will continue to use until they are drug-dependent or addicted.

No matter what the case, abusive use needs to be considered a warning sign. Family intervention should be discussed and possibly pursued, earlier rather than later.

> *Information is not knowledge.*
>
> —*Albert Einstein*

Q *Is it true that the more educated a person is, the less likely they are to become an addict?*

A. Yes.

Education about the potential dangers of alcohol or drug addiction is very important, and can help people avoid problems. Knowledge of the warning signs and awareness of one's genetic predisposition can also be catalysts for avoiding addiction. Still, because of the very subtle onset of dependency, even the most educated people in society can become addicted.

I know a man who graduated from Harvard. Close to ten years later, he lost his practice, and almost lost his wife and family as well, due to his addiction. He was a clinical psychologist at the time. He now has over twelve years in recovery.

Addiction affects almost all groups of people regardless of age, race, economic status, gender, culture, or level of education—from Yale to jail. Nevertheless, I think that education on the topic of addiction/dependency is the most powerful tool we have to combat the problem.

Q *Is it true that the chances for addiction are greater the earlier use starts?*

A.   Yes.

Research and statistics confirm that the earlier a person begins using substances, the more likely they are to become dependent on them. A thirteen-year-old who begins using drugs and alcohol is four times more likely to become an alcoholic or drug addict than someone who waits until they are twenty-one years old to experiment.

The adolescent brain is a work in progress. When alcohol or drug use begins at thirteen, the brain will learn to expect these substances as part of its development. We also know that this phase of life—adolescence—is a difficult time for many teens. The availability of drugs, peer pressure, a strong desire to be accepted, and curiosity are all enticements to experiment. This stage of life is also when teens learn coping skills, learn how to handle emotions such as anger and frustration, and begin to mature sexually. Teens often use drugs and alcohol to relieve anxiety and stress during this transition from childhood to adulthood. All of this can be a setup for continued use. Most young people will go through this phase and mature to become social drinkers and non-drug users. Some, a growing percentage, will continue to depend on substances to handle life's problems. Many in this group will become addicted.

Parents, or those close to teens, should do all they can to delay experimentation. It has been said that kids spell love T-I-M-E. The more time we can spend with our teens is time well spent.

CAN IT HAPPEN?

> *It takes only one drink to get me drunk.*
> *The trouble is, I can't remember if it's the*
> *thirteenth or the fortieth.*
>
> —*George Burns*

Q *Can someone develop a chemical dependency problem later in life?*

A. *Yes.*

Often men and women who never had an addiction or drug dependency problem can find themselves vulnerable. In fact, now there are treatment centers and recovery groups specifically for people age fifty-five and older.

There are several reasons why dependency may develop in seniors. Men and women who had successful careers or busy lives raising children can feel lonely or depressed in retirement. Often a person's entire identity and self-worth were wrapped up in the roles they fulfilled during their younger years. If the loss of that identity and self-worth leads to depression or lack of purpose, the once social drinker may now drink more frequently.

The aging body will not be able to handle alcohol the way it once did. The effect of alcohol on an older person's already unsteady physical balance can make them more prone to accidents. Also, alcohol mixed with other prescription medications can cause mental disorientation. When this condition plays out behind the wheel of a car, the consequences can be tragic.

Aging usually brings about added health concerns, such as sleeping problems, arthritis pain and a host of other age-related afflictions that require prescription medications. Over time, a person may build a tolerance to some of these, such as pain medications. As various medications are combined, the abuser may not be aware of what is happening to his or her body. On the other hand, they may try to hide the problem because of embarrassment or shame. For these folks, intervention will take on a completely different look and feel. In fact, the children may need to be the ones to intervene for their mom or dad.

Q *Can a person just cut down on their drinking?*

A.   *Yes, a person can just cut down.*

But not if the person is an alcoholic or drug addict. When we are talking about cutting down, the implication is that the person has the ability to control how much he uses without going overboard or having problems. Lack of control is perhaps the biggest sign of addiction. For the dependent person, alcohol or drugs now have control. At this point, it is often the person's stubborn pride that keeps them from seeing the problem. Whether you are asking this question of yourself or if you are thinking of someone close to you, it is a red flag—a warning sign. Social drinkers rarely, if ever, need to think about being able to control how much they drink.

DO YOU HAVE TO?

Q *Do you have to believe in God to attend AA meetings?*

A.   No.

There are mainly two different kinds of AA meetings, *open* and *closed*. An open meeting is for anyone who wants to attend. The closed meeting is only for people who believe they have an alcohol/drug dependency problem. Neither of these meetings requires a belief in God. The twelve steps refer to a higher power or God "as you understand him," but during meetings and in AA literature, the mention of any particular religion is discouraged. In this way, anyone can attend without feeling pressure to join a particular religion, belief system, or church. AA *does believe* that alcoholism/addiction is too powerful to overcome by self-will alone. The "higher power" or God referred to in the steps is benevolent, caring, loving, and wants to help men and women defeat their addictions. Often, men and women who do not believe in God, will simply use "The AA Group" as their higher power.

When I first started attending AA, I had no religious beliefs. All I had was a desire to quit using alcohol and drugs. *Sometimes a person will not even have the desire.* It is during times like this that the Higher Power (God) comes into a person's life—to do for a person, that which he cannot do alone.

Q *Do you have to stop seeing all your old friends in order to recover?*

A. *It depends.*

When I was first getting off alcohol and drugs, many of my old friends were just like me. I knew that being around drugs and being around people using them was a bad idea. Exposing myself to the wrong influences would have been a set-up for relapse. It wasn't easy to let go of some of my longstanding relationships. At the same time, though, I was meeting new people who were also in recovery. I quickly learned that my new lifestyle and old friends were kind of like oil and water—they just didn't mix.

After several weeks of sobriety, I started to see these old relationships in a different light. I tried to talk to some of my old friends about recovery. A few of them actually quit using. Others began to avoid me. I stayed busy concentrating on not using. It was a little depressing, in a way. I wanted so much to help them change, but many just weren't interested.

This is a difficult time for the recovering person. There is a sort of lag-time between leaving old unhealthy relationships and developing new and better ones. It doesn't happen overnight—but it will happen. Trust the process and trust God to provide. For myself, I knew what was at stake. I had to do this or soon return to the old life. The void in my social life was going to be filled one way or another. This is one more reason why groups are important. Recovery means making many changes, and some are more difficult than others.

I am including this story of "Jenny's Pearl Necklace" at the request of my wife Judy. It is one of her favorites—all about "letting go, and letting God." Time and time again Judy and I have found that once we were willing to trust God, He would surprise us with a blessing far beyond anything we would have dreamed. The story touches everyone in a different way—as we are all at different stages of our journey.

Jenny's Pearl Necklace

The cheerful girl with bouncy golden curls was almost five. Waiting with her mother at the checkout stand, she saw them: a circle of glistening white pearls in a pink foil box.

"Oh please, Mommy. Can I have them? Please, Mommy, please!" Quickly the mother checked the back of the little foil box and then looked back into the pleading blue eyes of her little girl's upturned face.

"A dollar ninety-five. That's almost $2. If you really want them, I'll think of some extra chores for you and in no time you can save enough money to buy them yourself." As soon as Jenny got home, she emptied her piggy bank and counted out 17 pennies. After dinner, she did more than her share of chores. She went to the neighbor, Mrs. McJames, and asked if she could pick dandelions for ten cents. On her birthday, Grandma gave her another new dollar bill and at last she had enough money to buy the necklace.

Jenny loved her pearls. They made her feel grown up. She wore them everywhere—Sunday school, kindergarten, even to bed.

Jenny had a very loving daddy and every night he would stop whatever he was doing and come upstairs to read her a story. One night when he finished the story, he asked Jenny, "Do you love me?"

"Oh yes, Daddy. You know that I love you."

"Then may I have your pearls?"

"Oh, Daddy, not my pearls. But you can have Princess—the white horse from my collection. Remember, Daddy? The one you gave me. She's my favorite."

"That's okay, honey. Daddy loves you. Good night." And he brushed her cheek with a kiss.

About a week later, after story time, Jenny's daddy asked again, "Do you love me?"

"Daddy, you know I love you."

"Then will you give me your pearls?"

"Oh, Daddy, not my pearls. But you can have my baby doll. The brand new one I got for my birthday.

"That's okay, Honey. Sleep well. God bless you, little one. Daddy loves you." And as always, he brushed her cheek with a gentle kiss. Several days later, when Jenny's father came in to read her a story, Jenny was sitting on her bed and her lip was trembling. "Here, Daddy," she said, and held out her hand. She opened it and her beloved pearl necklace was inside. She let it slip into her father's hand.

With one hand her father held the plastic pearls and with the other he pulled out of his pocket a blue velvet box.

Inside of the box were real, genuine, beautiful pearls. He had had them all along. He was waiting for Jenny to give up the cheap stuff so he could give her the real thing.

So it is with our Heavenly Father. He is waiting for us to be willing to give up things in our lives so he can give us beautiful treasure.

God only wants you to have the best.

—Author Unknown, Source Unknown

Real
Stories,
Real
People

Real Stories, Real People

Never give up hope. I've been inspired over and over by the testimonies of those who have lived through the nightmare of addiction and managed to regain control of their lives. When you find yourself discouraged and ready to give up hope for someone you love, you may find these accounts to be the inspiration you need.

Our first story comes to us from a woman I recently helped coach through some very tough times. Little did I realize just *how tough.* I like to try to remember, "you never know just what someone might be going through . . ."

Although it was difficult for her to revisit these experiences, she did a superb job recounting the past and sharing her insights. But for the grace of God and her wise but painful decisions about how to handle Dan, she could so easily have had one more funeral to attend.

Dan's Story
A Mother's Painful Lessons Learned

It is difficult to think back on the story of my son, Daniel, and his addiction. It is hard to experience once again the pain of that time in my life. I do so—that I may remember more clearly the lessons I have learned and perhaps help someone else who may be facing this destructive disease.

Although Dan's father and I divorced when Dan was seven, it was in

Dan's early middle school years when my family started on his painful path of using. Perhaps Dan's use started because there was more friction between his parents, or his best friend moved away in 6th grade, or that in six months time Dan went from a little boy to looking like he was eighteen years old. It really doesn't matter how it began, the truth is Dan used because he is an addict.

My relationship with my son was very strong and loving throughout his young life, so when there started to be some tension and fighting, it seemed normal; it was important that he "break" from his strong ties with his mom to search out his identification as a young man. I still think that was a reasonable explanation initially but I held on to that explanation long after I knew in my heart it was more than that.

My son was an athlete who excelled at all team sports. He had gone through puberty early which gave him an advantage of size and coordination. He was unassuming and coachable; his teams were successful and his teammates looked up to him. For whatever reasons, he was attracted to the wrong crowd. He said kids his age were boring and since he looked older, he gravitated to older kids.

In eighth grade his behavior became erratic. He would get angry in a split second over little things and he started punching walls and breaking chairs. He got into some minor trouble at school and at the end of his eighth grade summer, he and a friend stole a car. He went through the diversion program and participated in a restorative justice program. It seemed he really understood that he needed to change his ways.

Dan's first year of high school had many successes in academics and sports. Socially, he still had friends his age but once again, the older crowd was becoming a big part of his life. Toward the end of his freshman year something changed and he started shutting me out of his life again. At the time I knew it was a red flag but could not convince his dad or his counselor that he was using.

Sophomore year was difficult. Dan would not speak to me, he lived full-time with his dad and was spiraling down. He was in therapy off and on with someone who was highly respected in the community and credible as an adolescent counselor. I kept insisting that I thought Dan's behavior was indicative of substance abuse, but no one agreed.

In February, Dan came to my house after school drunk with marks on his arms from hurting himself. He said he wanted to die. I called the police, Dan went to the ER and then was released to a psychiatric hospital. When he was to be dismissed, he said he would not do any outpatient care and his therapist recommended a wilderness program. I knew I couldn't watch him 24-7 and I knew that is what he needed. He was there for two and a half months—which gave me some hope and some sleep, but the program did not emphasize the disease of addiction. Dan had no 12-step skills, no understanding of his disease and the first weekend home he went to a party and came home totally smashed.

I don't remember specifics of junior year. It was a fog of sleepless nights, days and nights of not knowing where he was or what he was doing or who he was with. Dan's dad was still in denial and refused to address the use issues. *Most high school kids drink and get in trouble, right? This is just normal high school stuff*—was the response I would get from so many people. I knew it wasn't; I knew Dan was one of those people who could not drink alcohol. I heard rumors about the people he was friends with and some of the criminal things they were doing. And I was torn about what I should do. I consulted many different therapists and was told there was nothing I could do. I called the police, I called a parole officer whose son struggled with the same issues, I talked to friends. It was the most frustrating, helpless, depressing time of my life. I would wake in the middle of the night in panic. *Was my son dead somewhere? Was he lying passed out in the freezing cold? If I did something now, would I save his life?* I would call his phone, not expecting him to pick up, but believing that it might wake him and keep him from dying. It was the most stressful and hopeless time of Dan's addiction for me. He ended up in the psychiatric hospital in February. Again, I asked the professionals if this could be a result of using and they said maybe, but they were looking at mental illness diagnoses.

In the summer after his junior year, my family experienced a tragedy. My oldest daughter's husband was killed by an impaired driver. It was devastating to the whole family and a turning point for Dan and me. Dan, of course, stepped up his use. He started using hard drugs and dropped out of school. For me, I had to turn my attention to my daughter and granddaughter. It forced me to "let go" of Dan's use and abuse issues and give them to him to figure out. I still prayed that he would live and choose to live clean and sober *but I stopped trying to make it happen.* My response changed from "You have to stop doing this to yourself or you will die" to "I pray that you choose to live life clean and sober and let me know what I can do to help you." I was consumed with grief over the loss of my son-in-law and with the need to help my daughter as a single parent. I had to prioritize my use of energy with a full-time job, my twenty-seven year old widowed daughter, my fatherless granddaughter, my fifteen year old daughter, and my using addict son. I just didn't have the energy to continue worrying about him the same way I had been. I had to "let it go" and trust that he would figure it out.

Dan expressed survivor guilt after his brother-in-law was killed, thinking *he was the one who messed up, he was the one who caused so much pain to the family and he was the one who deserved to die.* He ended up in jail the summer after what should have been his graduation from high school. He had stolen a car again and was writing checks on his dad's account. When he got out of jail he came to live with me amid promises of not using and following the terms of his probation. After a few months his use escalated to shooting heroin and he attended a 30 day treatment program in December. His sisters and I came to family week to support him in his recovery. We wanted to show him we cared, but we also were resentful that he was asking more of us. We hoped for the best for him this time, but we still saw signs that he didn't take full responsibility.

Most importantly, during these family sessions I gained clarity about what my boundaries needed to be and made a commitment to hold to them. If I suspected that he was high, I *would not* ask him to confirm or deny it, I would ask him to leave. He could not live in my house if he was using. And I learned to trust my intuition regarding whether he was and I did not need someone else to agree with me. I had the confidence to believe that I knew my son and his behavior well enough—to know when he was clean and when he was not. I also came to the realization that there was nothing I could have done to keep my son-in-law from being killed and there was nothing I could do to keep my son alive if he was determined to die.

A few weeks after he "graduated" from rehab, he started using again. I told him I loved him and he was not following the rules we established. He needed to leave. When I came home from work I began to realize that he had been coming in the house through different windows. He had done this in the past just to get in, but this time was different. This time, he was coming in to steal from me. He stole gold jewelry, tools, and musical instruments. I went to pawn shops in town and was able to track down some of the items and get the names of the young men who had pawned them for Dan. With this information, I filed a police report. Although it was difficult to do, I was certain that my son was begging me to do something drastic. He was out of control and could not stop himself. *I was going to help him by keeping my boundaries.*

The next time I talked with Dan I gave him a choice. He could admit himself into a detox unit and make a commitment to staying clean and sober or I was going to file charges against him for theft. He choose detox. He worked with his probation officer on some different living situations after he detoxed, but one required a year commitment and one was not an option because Dan was on probation. Joe coached me through this trying time. I had read Joe's book and knew I needed to be clear about my boundaries and the consequences. When my son got out after 3 days of detoxing, once again, he got high. I told him to leave again. Joe had told me to tell Dan not to come back until after he was clean for 90 days. I told Dan that. Dan left the house and I broke down in tears.

The next day I called one of the counselors at the detox and told him that I kicked Dan out because he used. The counselor said *good*. I needed that support. I called Joe and asked if I should file charges, like I said I would. Joe reminded me that my son would not die of an overdose in jail. *I needed that reminder.* I needed the support of these recovery experts in order to do what I needed to do.

The next morning I went into the garage to let out the dog before I went to work. My son was sleeping there, huddled up next to the dog. It was one of the most heartbreaking sights for me. *How could it have come to this? My once sweet, loving boy—now a heroin addict who is living like a dog?* Again, I told him I loved him and the agreement we had was that if he used I would file charges. I told him that I would file charges after work. That afternoon I got a call from Dan's probation officer who said Dan had come and asked her to do something for him. He needed help. She called a Christian sober living home and Dan could come and live there, but needed to make a one year commitment. Dan agreed. I did not file charges that afternoon, but there is no doubt in my mind I would have. And I think there was no doubt in Dan's mind that day that I would have.

The relief I felt for the next few weeks was unbelievable. I woke up in the morning after a full night's sleep. I rested with the assurance that my son was in a safe and healthy place. The surrender that began when I turned my son's addiction over to him ended with complete relief. I couldn't talk with him the first month he was there and I was glad of that. I knew I could get hooked back in and I knew it would not be good for any of us.

I went to see him after about four weeks and he looked better than he had in the last year. My son looked like himself, talked to me with love and gentleness and wanted to stay where he was and be clean.

That was seven months ago and our relationship continues to re-build. I learned well that he was not trustworthy and I'm not sure how long it will take for me to believe what he says. I have always believed *in* him and I still do. The lying, deceit, and stealing destroyed the foundation of our relationship. That is a reality of the using addict's life. I imagine it will take as many years to rebuild my trust as he spent destroying my trust.

When I look back, it's hard to say if I did the right thing or not all those years. I have come to believe that life is a process and *I can only know what I know when I know it.* I am grateful that Dan is where he is now and I relish each day of his sobriety. I pray that he chooses life each day and not the death that comes with using. Recovery is a marathon and he is in the first mile. I am clear that my role is to support and not enable, to have clear boundaries and to love him. Everything else is up to him.

I am grateful today not for the pain of these last few years of my life but for the lessons I have learned from dealing with that pain. Those lessons include learning to trust my intuition, learning to set and maintain clear boundaries with love and kindness, learning acceptance for what is, and trusting the judgment of people like Joe.

Angela's Story
Somewhere Over the Rainbow

Angela is a Native American who grew up on a reservation in Arizona. She has beautiful long hair, big, soulful brown eyes and a glowing smile. Two of her older brothers died from alcoholism-related incidents, along with her mother, whom she loved dearly—all before she reached the age of sixteen. She followed in their footsteps—and found herself trapped in a lifestyle that revolved around alcohol and drugs. She started with pot, but very quickly found herself using all kinds of drugs as well. Angela dropped out of school and left for San Diego, hoping that a change in environment would help to get her life on track.

But her hopes spiraled downward, and her drinking and drug use reached the point of severe addiction, which left her homeless in San Diego. For the next twenty-four years, Angela struggled. Sometimes she survived by raiding dumpsters for food and by exchanging sexual favors for drugs. At the age of eighteen, she became pregnant and went through the heartbreak of giving up her child. Sometimes she spent the night in a shelter, but she told me that places like this could be more dangerous than spending the night on the street. Occasionally she would attend an AA meeting, often just for the free coffee and to use the bathroom.

While sitting in a park one Sunday morning she met a couple of women who offered to help her. This was the turning point in her life. Now close to forty, Angela was—from all outward appearances—worn out and beyond hope. Nevertheless, she had never given up her dream of a better life. These two women, who were in recovery themselves, sparked the embers of hope deep within Angela and began to help her climb out of her pit of despair.

She began attending all the 12-step groups she could find, took advantage of the support and advice that was offered and totally surrendered to her disease. Within a few weeks, her life began to improve. With substances no longer controlling her, her past hopes and dreams once again emerged. Angela began to look and feel better, and the sparkle that had been lost since her childhood returned to her eyes. With the help of her newfound friends, she gained strength and clarity, and slowly began to believe in herself. Angela had her ups and downs as she struggled to live her life substance-free.

Common, everyday events were brand-new experiences for her. At first, learning to get out of bed in the morning, eat breakfast and go to a group meeting were all goals to be achieved. For the first time since childhood she experienced life raw—the highs and the lows, totally without the veil of substances. An innocent look or random comment from someone was often an occasion for a heated argument. On the other hand, a friendly "hello" from the grocery store clerk could produce tremendous happiness and gratitude for life itself. When she felt frustrated and ready to give up, Angela leaned on the support of friends who had been through the same thing, as well as the God she was also building a relationship with.

She found a part-time job, shared an apartment with some other women (also in recovery), received help that enabled her to complete her high-school education, and attended many group meetings. Her enthusiasm for life and self-confidence emerged. Within a few years, Angela had received her GED, found a full-time job with a good salary, and enrolled in night classes at a community college.

Angela finished college, went on to graduate from law school and is now an attorney specializing in Native American rights. When she speaks to groups today, she notes that attending recovery meetings enabled her to overcome her fear of public speaking and gave her the confidence to pursue her dreams.

Angela's story is a true inspiration, and serves as illustration that no person is beyond hope. Recovery is available to anyone who will surrender to this disease and be willing to reach out for help.

Lonnie's Story
Love at First Sight

Years ago, when crack cocaine was becoming a big problem, I met Lonnie at a support group. He was married and had a ten-year-old son he adored. Lonnie, a burly young man, grew up in Chicago. Four years prior to our meeting, he was your "white collar" average office worker who enjoyed coming home from his job to barbeque, enjoy a beer, spend time with his wife, and play catch with their son.

One night a buddy from his softball team introduced him to crack cocaine. Reluctant at first, but nevertheless curious, he tried it. It was *love at first sight.* For a while he occasionally used it on weekends, but soon he started to binge. According to his wife, he would disappear for days at a time and his life rapidly unraveled. He would take all their money and buy several vials of crack, rent a room in a cheap motel and smoke until it was all gone. When his ATM card wouldn't work any longer, he would return home. Lonnie lost his job and began working temporary manual labor jobs to earn what he could when he was able. At one point, he said, he went for a few months without using—all on his own, using his willpower. Life was not easy; getting through even one day seemed a never-ending task. Then one day he just left work to go buy more crack. He talks about the experience as kind of surreal. Everything was going fine, no problem or reason to do it; he just got up and left.

After a binge of several days, he was broke again. The drug dealer said he would supply him with more crack if he would be a lookout for him. For the next few weeks he lived in an old abandoned building in the middle of a dangerous, gang-ridden section of Chicago, where he smoked crack and watched people across the street standing in line to buy their drugs. He didn't shower or shave, and rarely ate anything. He literally turned into a different person. Sick, dirty, tired and broken, he arrived back home. His wife met him at the door with an ultimatum—get help, or leave and never come back.

With the help of volunteers at a local shelter, he entered treatment and began his journey back. It took Lonnie a few slips and a second treatment in another facility before his recovery was successful. He has been straight for eight years now, and support groups are still a big part of his life. He said that trying to quit on his own would never have worked for him. Although he had the support of his family at the time he tried to quit by himself, he realizes there is no substitute for the camaraderie and true understanding of people who have been there. *He credits his new life to the grace of God and the people God used to open his eyes.*

Judy's Story
Secrets

Judy grew up in the small college town of Clinton, NY. She learned to ski, went to summer camp, had many friends, and received good grades in school. Most observers would say that Judy was the typical all-American girl with a promising future. But one particular pastime began to overshadow everything else. Judy and her high-school friends often spent weekends attending sports events, which were usually followed by keg parties—always held in a different secret location, down a country road. By the age of sixteen, she had already discovered that *when you drink, you drink to get drunk.* That's what everyone did (or so she thought).

Judy's life went along as planned—college, graduation, perfect career, marriage, vacations, and a storybook house. Although there was so much *right* about her life, from the age of sixteen to the age of twenty-nine, Judy lived for her next drink. The years passed quickly, and for as long as she could remember, her life secretly revolved around drinking. She would organize her days centered on when she would be able to *reward herself* with a bottle or two of wine or (later) something stronger. Drinking was a treat—something to make life more fun, to celebrate, to make cleaning the house more *fun*. Today, she would be referred to as a "high-functioning alcoholic."

Although the signs were obvious to people close to Judy, she was convinced that she had everything under control. She actually believed that no one really knew how much she looked forward to her *rewards*. This lifestyle continued for years with occasional, but increasing, blackouts and other incidents. She convinced herself that if she was able to do a great job at work, maintain a perfect house and garden, entertain guests, travel for her career, take exciting vacations and look nice, then everything was normal and there was no problem. She had never known anyone with an alcohol problem before, so she had no idea what a problem even looked like. All of the couples that she knew would drink and get drunk—just like her, she thought. Life was good, until Judy began to suspect that something was terribly wrong.

I started to hide how much I drank. I would drink before events so people wouldn't think I was consuming so much. I took bottles of wine, and later, vodka, to my job, in my (very large) purse. When I was traveling for work, I would order room service (I always asked for two glasses) before going out to dinner with a group. On these trips, I would take a plastic jug in my suitcase filled with vodka and measure off how much I could drink per day in order to maintain normalcy (so my hands would not shake). This was my medicine. I discovered that if I drank first thing in the morning,

I would feel great by the time I walked out the door for work; a few drinks, a shower, some Visine and mouthwash, and I was ready for my day. I began to drive home at lunchtime to drink, so I could keep the exact right amount of alcohol in my system to get through the afternoon. At the same time, I would replenish my hiding places throughout the house—to get me through the evening without my husband knowing my secret.

She now realized that her body had come to expect the drug, and without it, she would go into withdrawal. She was terrified that someone might notice her hand shaking as she took notes or drank out of a glass during a meeting at work. Her life revolved around maintaining the precise amount of alcohol in her system, and too little or too much caused major problems.

After more than two years of attempting to maintain this façade, Judy faced her moment of decision. Because of repeated incidents during work, her bosses called her into the office and gave her an ultimatum. They told her, "We've never dealt with this problem before, so we aren't sure what to do, but you need to do something about your drinkin problem or you will lose your job. You can either go to treatment, or you can talk to someone from AA. Here's a phone number."

Judy had known for some time that *her drinking days were numbered* and she was just waiting for something bad to happen. This was it. She had reached her bottom. She had already lost her husband—he had left months earlier. That had been troubling, yet because of the hold alcohol had on her, she was relieved that she no longer had to hide her drinking at home. Her friends and parents tried to intervene, however, her bosses' ultimatum was a severe wake-up call, and she knew that her drinking days finally needed to be over if she were to survive. Without her career, she would be stripped of the very thing that she was most proud of; she would be completely alone, with no money. Most alcoholics aren't as lucky as Judy. She didn't have to lose her home or her job, as some do, before she "hit bottom."

Still, Judy didn't know exactly *how* she was going to stop drinking, since she really had no desire to stop; she just knew that she *had* to. She was afraid and very alone. After evaluating recovery options, she chose not to go to treatment, thinking that if she went away, then everyone at work would know about her problem.

She called the number her bosses gave her and the AA person spoke about a meeting in her neighborhood. She scratched down the address and time on a piece of paper. Judy doesn't remember how, but she arrived there that night.

The people were all so nice, but I wasn't quite ready to quit. I went back and drank for several more days. Then, for some (divine) reason, I found myself back at another meeting. By the grace of God, I somehow listened to what these people had to say, and kept coming back. I know it wasn't my strength that saw me through. It really was a miracle—and I didn't drink.

Following that, everything improved for Judy. She learned to take things "one day at a time." For the first few months, her life consisted of going to work during the day and attending a meeting every evening. It has now been over twenty-five years since the day her bosses intervened. She hasn't had a drink since.

In one way it seems like another lifetime, and in another way it seems like just yesterday. It's good to never forget. I have too much to lose.

Now, hiking, gardening, and spending time with her children, her pets, and her husband are a part of life that she doesn't take for granted. She has a healthy respect for alcohol and knows that it is no longer an option for her.

Judy's addiction was very real and will always be with her. On the other hand, her recovery is very real as well. Today she shares her story with men and women who are interested.

I can see that God carried me when I didn't have the strength or willpower on my own. I didn't want to quit and somehow He came into my life and provided me with that desire. I know that desire did not come from within me. Only later, was I able to look back and see how He worked this miracle for me.

Brian's Story
The Real Deal

Sadly, many people released from prison end up returning. Let me tell you about a friend of mine who beat the odds. Brian didn't like prison. In fact, he said he despised everything about it. When he was released after serving a three-year sentence, he told me he was never going back. This is what most people say when they are released. But Brian meant it.

His success story is one that helps me to keep the faith when it comes to repeat offenders. For a time, he was stuck in the typical cycle: he was in and out of jail before he eventually went to prison for three years. I had worked with him many times over the years. He had received five DUIs and refused to go to any treatment or group meetings unless it was court-ordered. I even visited him a few times when he was in DOC (Department of Corrections; a nice name for *prison*).

For Brian, a three-year prison sentence was a rude awakening. He finally realized his alcohol and drug use was out of control. When he left DOC, he had a felony on his record, making it more difficult to get a good job. Determined to be successful, Brian said it didn't matter where he worked—even if it was at a fast-food restaurant, he'd do it. He didn't have to, though, because he ended up getting a job working construction. While in prison, he attended AA meetings, bible studies and drug classes and continued going to meetings after he was released.

For a while he lived with his aunt, but soon made enough money to get his own apartment. It wasn't much, but it was the first time in years he had his own place to sleep. Slowly, he was making a better life for himself. Because of his past DUIs, he didn't have a driver's license, so he would take a bus or get a ride to work. Brian didn't let any obstacles keep him from excelling and overcoming his past.

He had worked construction as a teen, and knew a lot about masonry, and after just a few months he was promoted to foreman. That first year of life out of prison consisted of working six days a week, attending his newfound church, twelve-step meetings, and finding time to sleep when he could. Brian was able to save some money, and when he got his driver's license back he proudly bought a new truck. He tells me this was exactly what he needed. He gradually gained confidence in himself and started enjoying his new life. Each step of determination allowed him to take back some of the privileges addiction had stolen.

Brian now helps others who are in the same situation. As you will often hear from those in recovery, supporting others is a source of strength for a recovering person and adds meaning to their life. Brian doesn't want to see anyone defeated by this disease and is a great role model. He follows a rule that works for him: If it's illegal, immoral, or irresponsible, don't do it. This guy is the *real deal*. I don't expect to see him going back to prison.

> **By endurance we conquer.**
> —*Ernest Shackleton*

Appendix B

Self Test

Self Test

Alcohol and Drug Addiction Self-Test:
Take this test for yourself or for someone you love.

Circle your response to the following statements:

Yes No   I use illegal substances, inhalants or non-prescribed
         doses of prescription drugs.

Yes No   I sometimes exceed the recommended dose of medica-
         tions, such as painkillers, diet pills, sleep aids, laxatives
         or cold medicines.

Yes No   I have been told I drink too much.

Yes No   Some of my closest friends are recreational drinkers
         or users.

Yes No   I sometimes hide my drinking or drug use from my
         family, my employer or law officers.

Yes No   In the past year, I have done some things I regret
         while I was drinking or using drugs.

Yes No   I've promised to quit, but I've broken that promise.

Yes   No   Drinking or using drugs isn't as much fun as
it used to be.

Yes   No   I sometimes drink or use drugs because I'm depressed
or lonely.

Yes   No   I sometimes drink or use drugs to cope with difficult
people or because I'm angry.

Yes   No   My drinking or drug use has caused financial problems.

Yes   No   My drinking or drug use has caused problems in my
closest relationships.

Yes   No   My drinking or drug use has caused problems at work
or school.

Yes   No   My drinking or drug use has caused problems with
my health.

Yes   No   My day revolves around daydreaming about getting,
using and recuperating from drinking or drug use.

Yes   No   I sometimes feel guilty for drinking or using drugs.

Yes   No   My family history includes people with problems with
alcohol or drugs.

Yes   No   When I've tried to quit, I experienced withdrawal
effects.

Yes   No   I need to drink or use drugs just to get going each day.

Yes   No   My life feels out of control because of my drinking or
              drug use.

Add up your totals and enter them into the "Yes" and "No" boxes.

_____Yes   _____No

- If you answered "yes" in response to **any** of these statements, you are at risk for problems with drinking or using drugs. Talk to a counselor or group facilitator now to gain information to stop any tendency toward further problems.

- If you answered "yes" in response to **3 or more** statements, you definitely have a problem with alcohol or drugs. Seek help from a counselor or support group immediately to get the help you need to repair the damage and get on the right track for your future.

- If you answered "yes" in response to **6 or more** statements, you definitely abuse drugs or alcohol, and you may well be an addict. You need immediate and comprehensive help to turn your life around. It's not too late. You need to see a physician and a drug and alcohol counselor, and you may need to be admitted to a treatment facility.

Appendix C

Resources

Online Resources*

General Info and Treatment:

www.ChangingLivesFoundation.org
Changing Lives Foundation. An informative site providing help for friends and family of addicts/alcoholics—with a focus on how individuals and families recover from these problems.

www.drug-addiction-support.org
Drug Addiction Support. News and current topics about drug addiction—including the latest books and DVD's for Addiction Recovery, along with resources to learn how to help your family deal with drugs.

www.naatp.org
National Association of Addiction Treatment Providers. Click on "Enter," then click on "Members." You can search by state or treatment center name.

www.sober.com
Sober.com. Committed to helping the addicted and families affected by drug abuse and drug addiction—to find rehabs, especially troubled teens. This site also includes various interesting venues for recovering people to connect with each other.

www.naadac.org
The Association for Addiction Professionals. A professional membership organization that serves counselors who specialize in addiction treatment.

www.hazelden.org
Hazelden. A site for individuals, families, and communities struggling with addiction to alcohol and other drugs. This nonprofit organization

helps people transform their lives by providing the highest quality treatment and continuing care services, education, research, and publishing products available today.

Twelve Step:

www.aa.org
Alcoholics Anonymous. A fellowship of men and women who share their experience, strength, and hope with each other so that they may solve their common problem and help others to recover from alcoholism (on the "Is AA for you?" page there are 12 questions to help you decide if you have a problem).

www.aagrapevine.org
AA Grapevine. Voice of Alcoholics Anonymous, The International Journal of AA, articles, stories, jokes, letters, subscriptions since 1944.

www.12step.org
12Step.org. Information and tools for working the 12-step program.

www.aa.org/bigbookonline
Read the AA Big Book online. Complete text of "Alcoholics Anonymous" also known as "The Big Book" is available in English, French, and Spanish.

www.anonpress.org/phone
AA Intergroup. Telephone Numbers, USA.

Christian Recovery:

www.addiction2recovery.com
addiction2recovery. reality.connection.change. Addiction recovery materials along with gripping videos of real people's stories of change and recovery.

www.celebraterecovery.com
Celebrate Recovery. A Christ-centered program ministering to those who struggle with hurts, hang-ups, habits or addictions.

Intervention:

www.a-i-r.com
Addiction Intervention Resources (AIR). A national organization of professional intervention specialists, counselors and consultants that provide fast and effective crisis management services through a proven protocol of education, action and healing. AIR addiction consultants can be reached at any time.

www.lovefirst.net
Love First. Professional interventionists, Jeff and Debra Jay, authors of *Love First*, published by Hazelden. Books. Videos, professional intervention, recovery mentoring and many free resources. Questions answered without charge. Interventionists nationwide.

Alcohol/Drugs:

www.nida.nih.gov
National Institute on Drug Abuse. NIDA's mission is to lead the nation in bringing the power of science to bear on drug abuse and addiction.

www.samhsa.gov
Substance Abuse & Mental Health Services Administration SAMHSA. Provides info on the prevention of substance abuse, alcohol and drug addiction, treatment, and mental health services.

www.ncadd.org
National Council on Alcoholism and Drug Dependence, Inc. (NCADD). Provides education, information, help, and hope to the public. It advocates prevention, intervention, and treatment through a nationwide network of affiliates.

www.niaaa.nih.gov
National Institute on Alcohol Abuse and Alcoholism. Provides current publications, research and news on alcohol addiction.

www.aca-usa.org
American Council on Alcoholism. More helpful information on intervention, problems surrounding alcohol abuse, self-tests, and other resources.

www.drugfree.org/Portal/Stories
The Partnership for a Drug-Free America. Personal, real-life stories of recovery.

www.anonymousone.com
AA, Al-Anon, find sober living homes, sober clubs, conferences, events, roundups, treatment centers, central offices, stories & articles of recovery, books & gifts for sobriety, daily meditations and much more.

Tobacco:

www.tobaccofacts.org/tob_truth/index.html
Tobacco Facts. Extensive information on smoking and the tobacco industry.

Online Communities/ Support:

www.friendsofbill.net
FOB (Friends of Bill). A social network specifically designed for alcoholics and addicts. Connect with new friends from all over the world who are just like you.

www.intherooms.com
In the Rooms. The premier, most comprehensive online social network for the recovery community worldwide. For the 23 hours a day you're not at a meeting, in the Rooms has many of the most popular 12-Step fellowships as groups for you to become a member of. In here you'll find great discussions, great people, resources, and archives.

www.facesandvoicesofrecovery.org

Faces and Voices of Recovery. Dedicated to changing public perceptions of recovery, promoting effective public policy in Washington and in all 50 states, and demonstrating that recovery is working for millions of Americans.

Family Support:

www.theantidrug.com

Parents. The Anti-Drug. Extensive amount of info, advice, resources specifically written for parents.

www.al-anon.org

Al-Anon/Alateen (which includes Alateen for younger members) offers hope and help to families and friends of alcoholics.

www.ola-is.org

Online Al-Anon Outreach. Information about online Al-Anon Family Groups and links to meetings on the Internet.

www.loveandlogic.com

Love and Logic. Helpful articles, simple and practical techniques to help parents and teachers have less stress and more fun while raising responsible kids.

Pain Management:

www.painmed.org/advocacy/ama_advocacy.html

The American Academy of Pain Medicine (AAPM) is the medical specialty society representing physicians practicing in the field of *Pain Medicine*.

Nutrition & Fitness:

www.cspinet.org/nah/index.htm

Nutrition Action. The largest-circulation health newsletter in North America providing reliable information on nutrition and health.

www.alcoholicsvictorious.org/faq/nutrition.html
Alcoholics Victorious. A (Christian-based) collection of articles that detail the effects of diet and nutrition on addiction recovery.

www.nutrition.gov
Nutrition Info—Dept. of Health and Human Services.

www.fitness.gov
Fitness Info—Dept. of Health and Human Services.

www.getfit.samhsa.gov
GetFit.SAMHSA. An interactive workplace web site that provides you, your family, and colleagues with information about physical health, mental health, drugs, and alcohol.

Recovery Radio:

www.drug-addiction-support.org/addiction-recovery-now.html
Recovery Now! A weekly radio program that discusses Alcoholism and Addiction recovery. Topics covered include: Causes, Symptoms, Intervention, Depression, Drug Therapies, 12-Step, Treatment Programs and much more. The format of the show is an informal roundtable discussion led by Addicition Chaplan Ned Wicker.

www.recoverycoasttocoast.org
Recovery Coast to Coast. Two hours of engaging dialogue, news updates and interviews around the topics of addiction, treatment, research and recovery.

Fun Stuff:

www.recoveryarts.com
RecoveryArts.com. A blog for and about the arts in recovery. By arts, we mean general expression: Recovery Poetry, Recovery Music, and Recovery Visual.

www.onerecovery.com
OneRecovery.com. A friendly and feature-rich online recovery community for alcohol, drug and eating disorder addiction.

www.theloiswilsonstory.com
The Lois Wilson Story. The first biography of the great American woman, wife of the man who co-founded Alcoholics Anonymous (AA)—a world-wide movement to save millions of families from the devastation of alcohol and drugs.

Assessments for yourself or others:

aa.org/lang/en/subpage.cfm?page=71
Is AA for you? 12 questions to help you decide if you have a problem.

www.drugfree.org/Intervention/Assessing
A site of drug assessments for all ages. Includes:

Tools to Assess Others:
How well do you know your teen? If you're a parent concerned about your teen's (12-18 years old) alcohol and/or drug use.

Al-Anon Quiz: If you're an adult concerned about another adult's (18 or older) drinking.

Drug Abuse Screening Test for Significant Others: If you're an adult concerned about another adult's (18 or older) drug use.

Self Assessment Tools:
CRAFFT Quiz: If you're a teen (12-17 years old) concerned about your own drug and/or alcohol use.

Alcohol Screener: If you're an adult (18 or older) concerned about your drinking.

Drug Abuse Screening Test: If you're an adult (18 or older) concerned about your drug use.

TO ACCESS THIS RESOURCE LIST ONLINE (Regularly updated):
www.ChangingLivesFoundation.org (click on RESOURCES)

*The list of organizations, professionals, and advisors (referred to hereafter as "advisors") is provided solely for informational purposes. Changing Lives Foundation does not endorse, and has not undertaken any independent investigation of the qualifications, credentials, experience, education, training, or proper licensing of, any advisor listed. Changing Lives Foundation does not have any direct or indirect input in any advice or services provided by any advisor listed in this book. Any person using contact information provided herein, to locate and select an advisor is strongly encouraged to inquire about the advisor's professional expertise, experience, licensing, and qualifications before engaging or hiring such a person or organization.

Visit our websites for articles and up to the minute information:

www.ChangingLivesFoundation.org

www.WhyDontTheyJustQuit.com

Other great resources from Changing Lives Foundation:*

- Audio Download and MP3 CD of Why Don't They Just Quit?
- Kindle and Nook eBook of Why Don't They Just Quit?
- 90 Min. DVD: Why Don't They Just Quit? Roundtable Discussion
- DVD: The 10 Toughest Questions Families and Friends Ask
  About Addiction and Recovery (perfect for group study)

*These items also available at Amazon.com, most libraries and online stores

Family Phone Counseling: with author/addiction counselor Joe Herzanek

Call for details: (303) 775.6493
or email: jherzanek@gmail.com

Join us on Facebook!:

- Why Dont They Just Quit? Book and DVD
- Changing Lives Foundation
- Changing Lives Foundation/Private Group: A supportive and loving place for families and friends of a person struggling with alcohol or drug abuse/addiction— to post, discuss and help each other. This is a closed group where anyone can join and safely post without fear of "the world" being able to see. You are NOT alone. Ask to join and someone will log you in!

I would love to hear from you!

Writing this book has been a fulfilling journey for me. Nevertheless, an even more rewarding experience would be to hear from my readers. How has this information impacted your life? Please write to me; with your permission, I would love to share in your recovery story.

Joe Herzanek
Changing Lives Foundation
1855 Gemini Ct.
Loveland, CO 80537

Do you know someone who doesn't know who to turn to, or who has lost hope? Give this book to a family member or friend in need of sound, practical advice from a certified substance abuse counselor who personally understands the powerful grip of addiction.

Order a gift today for someone at:
www.WhyDontTheyJustQuit.com